SO ... I SURVIVED THE

ZOMBIE
APOCALYPSE

AND ALL I GOT
WAS THIS PODCAST

D1588561

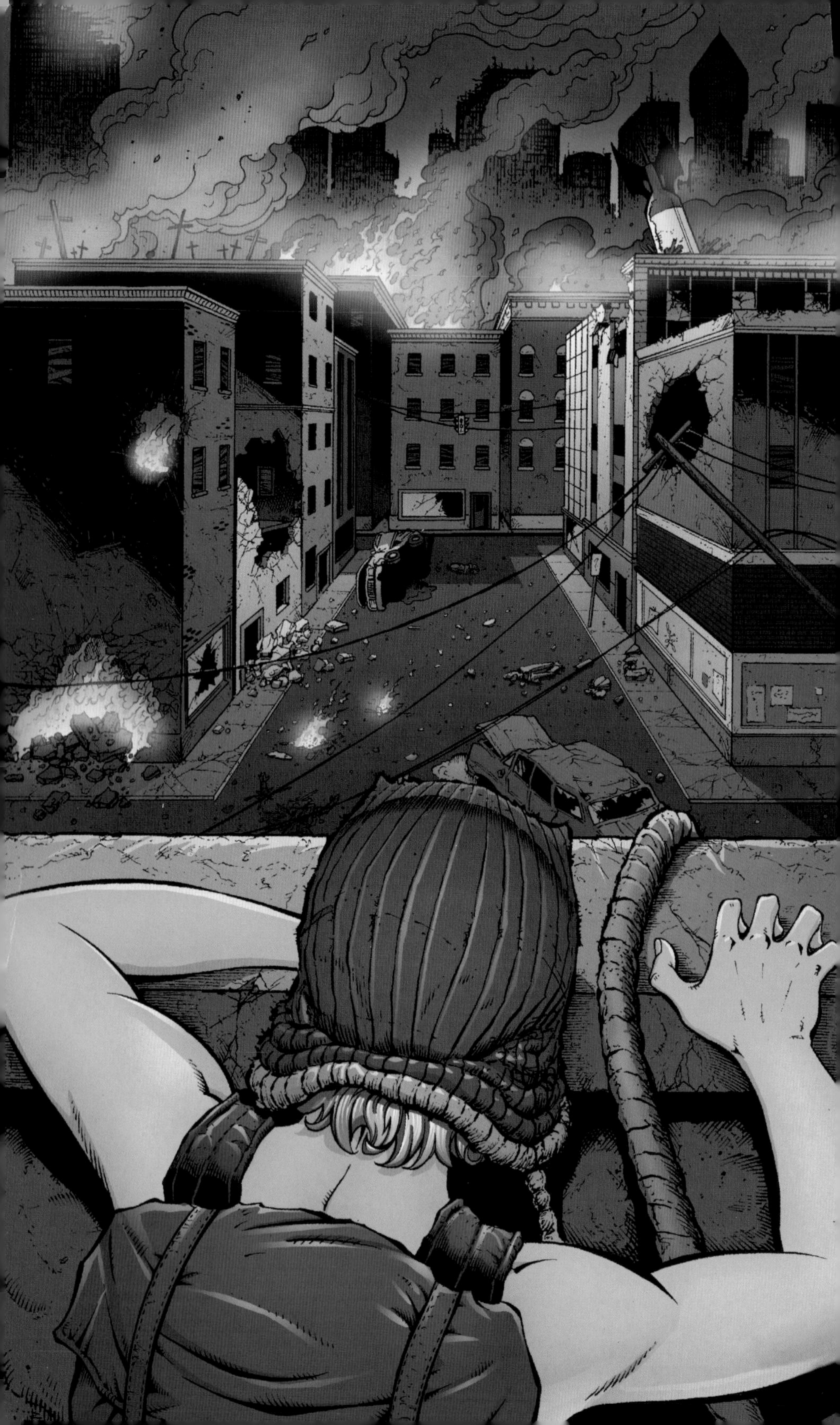

SO... I SURVIVED THE ZOMBIE APOCALYPSE AND ALL I GOT WAS THIS PODCAST™

Created by
**Jonathan Appel, Chris W. Freeman,
and Korey Hunt**

Written by
Chris W. Freeman and Korey Hunt

Art by
**Richard Bonk, Andrew Mangum,
Alan Kupperberg, Anthony Diecidue,
and Jerry Beck**

Colors by **Thomas Chu**
Letters by **Kel Nuttall**
Cover by **Melike Acar**

FOUNTAINDALE PUBLIC LIBRARY DISTRICT
300 West Briarcliff Road
Bolingbrook, IL 60440-2894
(630) 759-2102

Dark Horse Books

Editor
Daniel Chabon

Assistant Editor
Shantel LaRocque

Designer
Adam Grano

Publisher
Mike Richardson

SO . . . I SURVIVED THE ZOMBIE APOCALYPSE AND ALL I GOT WAS THIS PODCAST
© 2013 Slumber Vision Entertainment, LLC. Dark Horse Books® and the Dark Horse logo
are registered trademarks of Dark Horse Comics, Inc. All rights reserved. No portion of
this publication may be reproduced or transmitted, in any form or by any means, without
the express written permission of Dark Horse Comics, Inc. Names, characters, places, and
incidents featured in this publication either are the product of the author's imagination or are
used fictitiously. Any resemblance to actual persons (living or dead), events, institutions, or
locales, without satiric intent, is coincidental.

Published by Dark Horse Books
A division of Dark Horse Comics, Inc.
10956 SE Main Street
Milwaukie, OR 97222

DarkHorse.com

International Licensing: (503) 905-2377

To find a comics shop in your area, call the Comic Shop Locator Service
toll-free at: (888) 266-4226.

First edition: November 2013
ISBN 978-1-61655-217-6
10 9 8 7 6 5 4 3 2 1
Printed in China

Mike Richardson, President and Publisher | Neil Hankerson, Executive Vice President | Tom
Weddle, Chief Financial Officer | Randy Stradley, Vice President of Publishing | Michael
Martens, Vice President of Book Trade Sales | Anita Nelson, Vice President of Business
Affairs | Scott Allie, Editor in Chief | Matt Parkinson, Vice President of Marketing | David
Scroggy, Vice President of Product Development | Dale LaFountain, Vice President of
Information Technology | Darlene Vogel, Senior Director of Print, Design, and Production |
Ken Lizzi, General Counsel | Davey Estrada, Editorial Director | Chris Warner, Senior Books
Editor | Diana Schutz, Executive Editor | Cary Grazzini, Director of Print and Development
| Lia Ribacchi, Art Director | Cara Niece, Director of Scheduling | Tim Wiesch, Director of
International Licensing | Mark Bernardi, Director of Digital Publishing

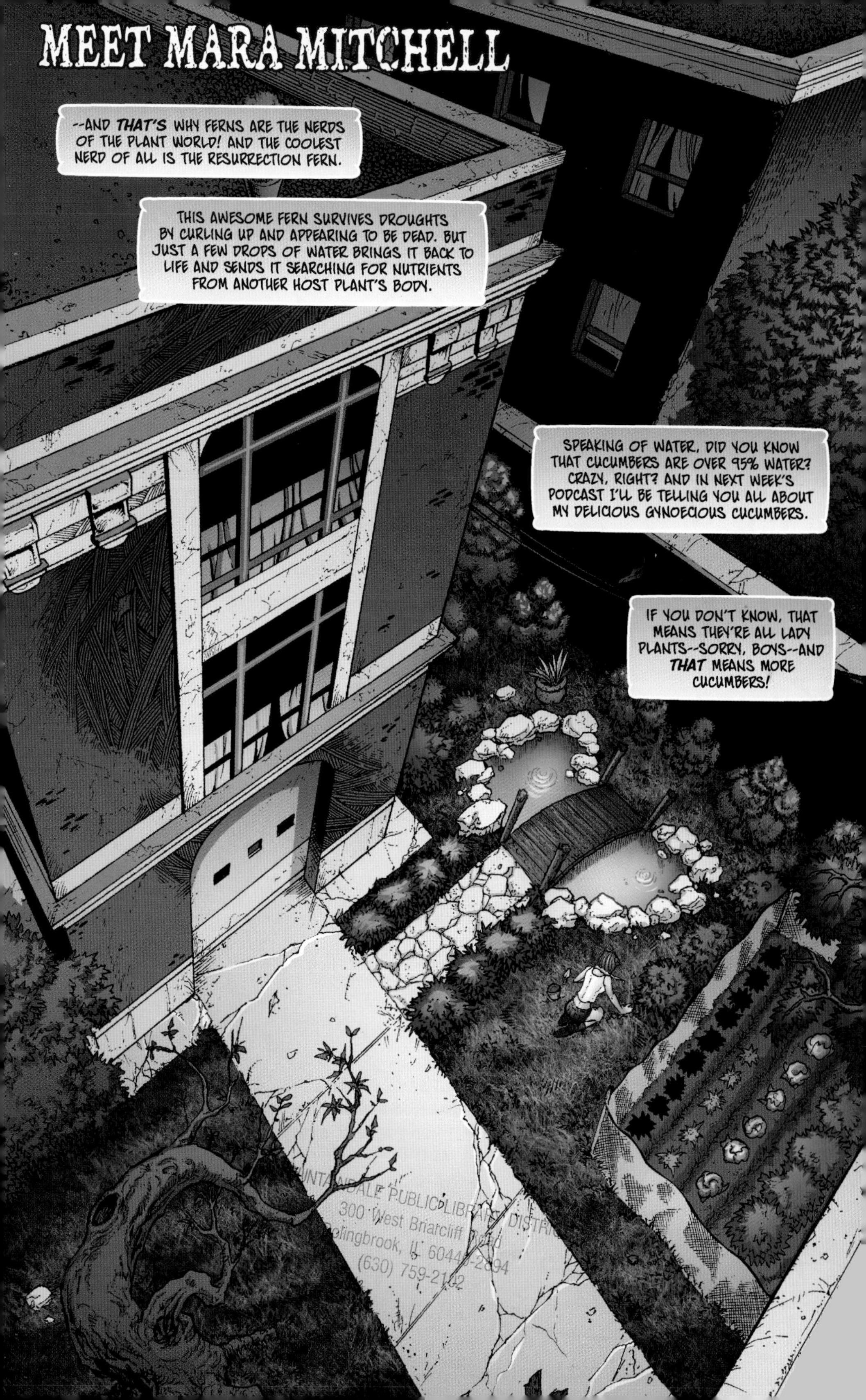
MEET MARA MITCHELL
--AND THAT'S WHY FERNS ARE THE NERDS OF THE PLANT WORLD! AND THE COOLEST NERD OF ALL IS THE RESURRECTION FERN.
THIS AWESOME FERN SURVIVES DROUGHTS BY CURLING UP AND APPEARING TO BE DEAD. BUT JUST A FEW DROPS OF WATER BRINGS IT BACK TO LIFE AND SENDS IT SEARCHING FOR NUTRIENTS FROM ANOTHER HOST PLANT'S BODY.
SPEAKING OF WATER, DID YOU KNOW THAT CUCUMBERS ARE OVER 95% WATER? CRAZY, RIGHT? AND IN NEXT WEEK'S PODCAST I'LL BE TELLING YOU ALL ABOUT MY DELICIOUS GYNOECIOUS CUCUMBERS.
IF YOU DON'T KNOW, THAT MEANS THEY'RE ALL LADY PLANTS--SORRY, BOYS--AND THAT MEANS MORE CUCUMBERS!

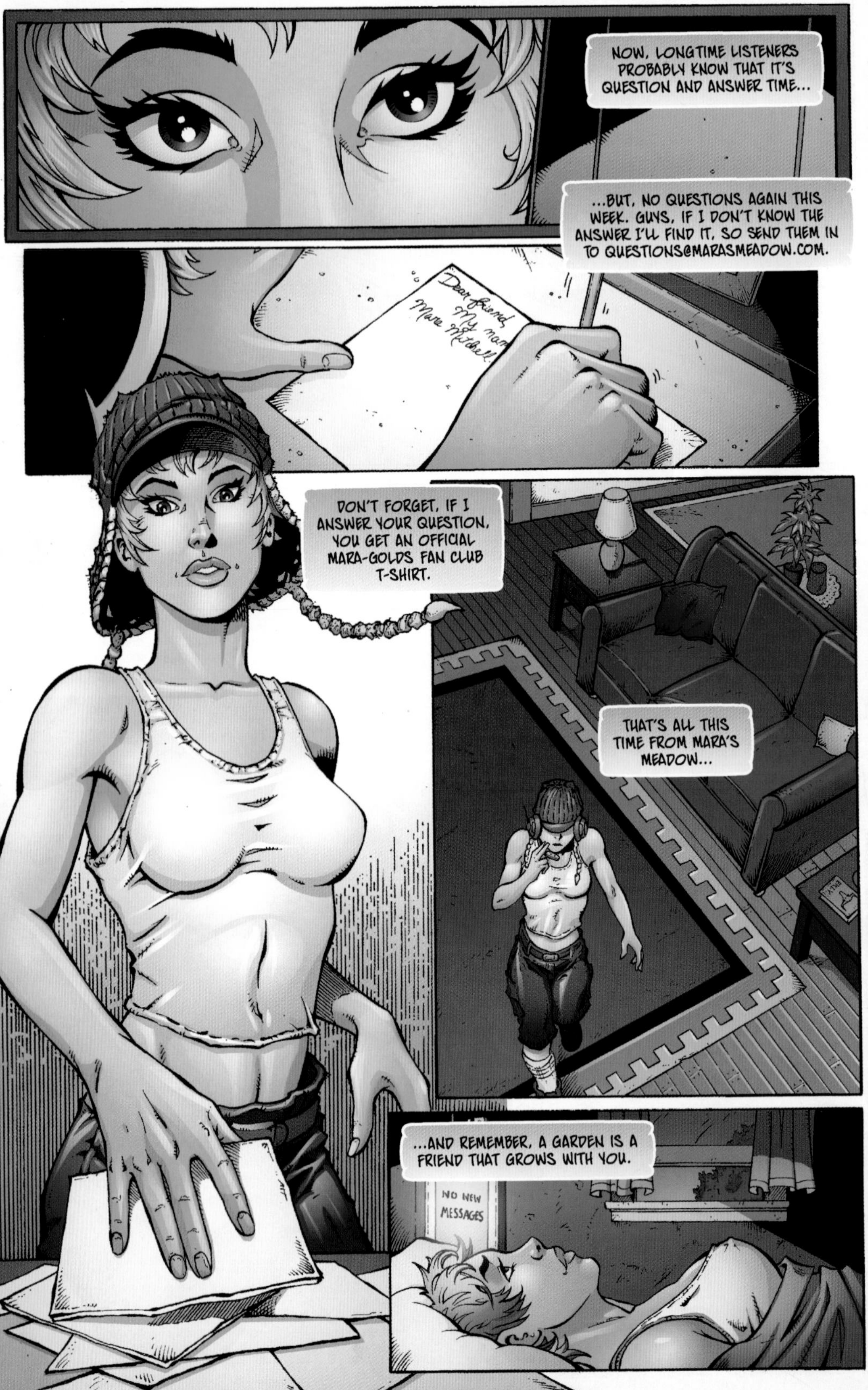
NOW, LONGTIME LISTENERS PROBABLY KNOW THAT IT'S QUESTION AND ANSWER TIME...
...BUT, NO QUESTIONS AGAIN THIS WEEK. GUYS, IF I DON'T KNOW THE ANSWER I'LL FIND IT, SO SEND THEM IN TO QUESTIONS@MARASMEADOW.COM.
Dear friend,
Mara Mitchell
DON'T FORGET, IF I ANSWER YOUR QUESTION, YOU GET AN OFFICIAL MARA-GOLDS FAN CLUB T-SHIRT.
THAT'S ALL THIS TIME FROM MARA'S MEADOW...
...AND REMEMBER, A GARDEN IS A FRIEND THAT GROWS WITH YOU.
NO NEW MESSAGES

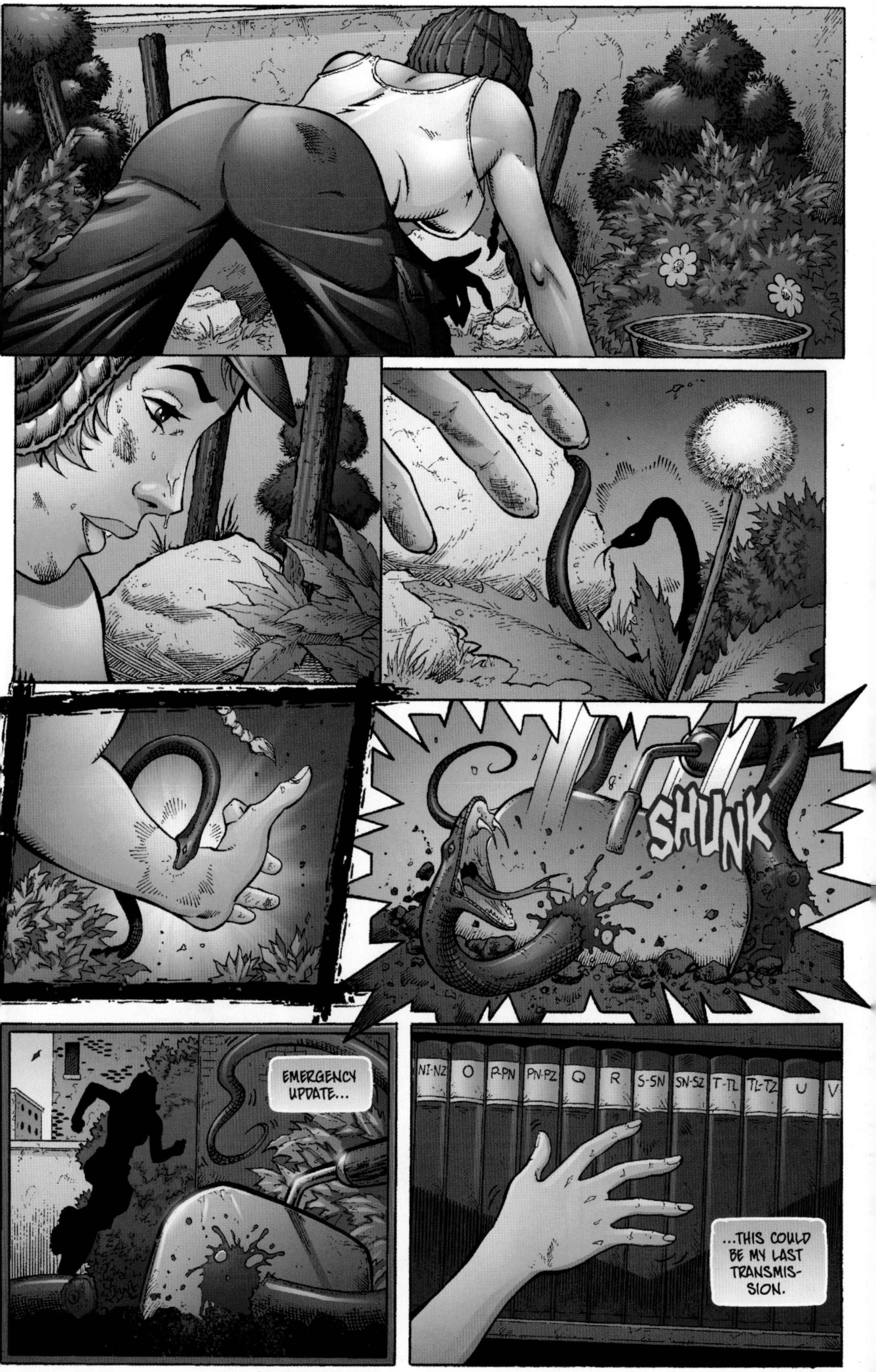
SHUNK
EMERGENCY UPDATE...
NI-NZ
O
P-PN
PN-PZ
Q
R
S-SN
SN-SZ
T-TL
TL-TZ
U
V
...THIS COULD BE MY LAST TRANSMIS-SION.

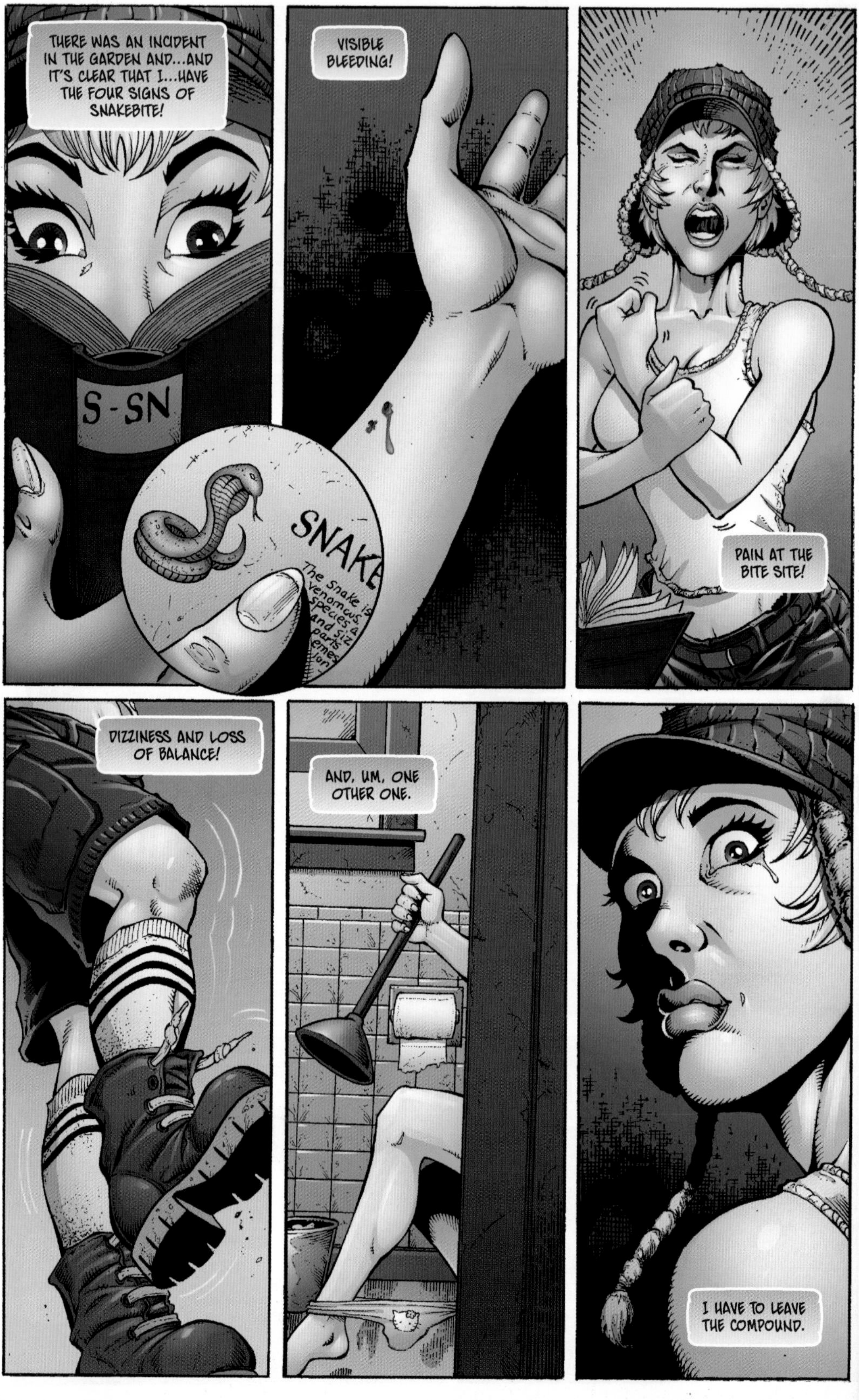
THERE WAS AN INCIDENT IN THE GARDEN AND...AND IT'S CLEAR THAT I...HAVE THE FOUR SIGNS OF SNAKEBITE!
S - SN
SNAKE
The Snake is
VISIBLE BLEEDING!
PAIN AT THE BITE SITE!
DIZZINESS AND LOSS OF BALANCE!
AND, UM, ONE OTHER ONE.
I HAVE TO LEAVE THE COMPOUND.

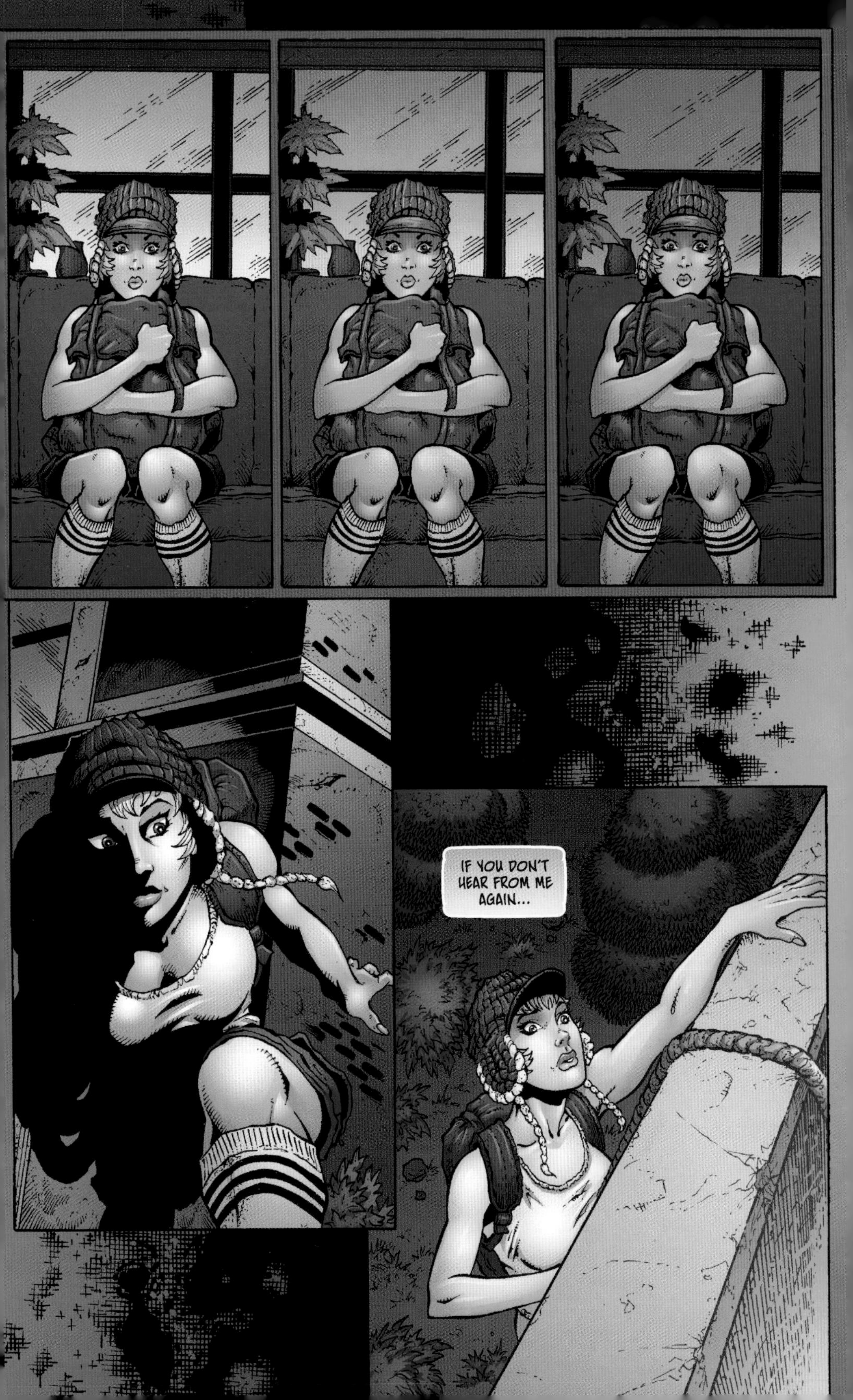
IF YOU DON'T HEAR FROM ME AGAIN...

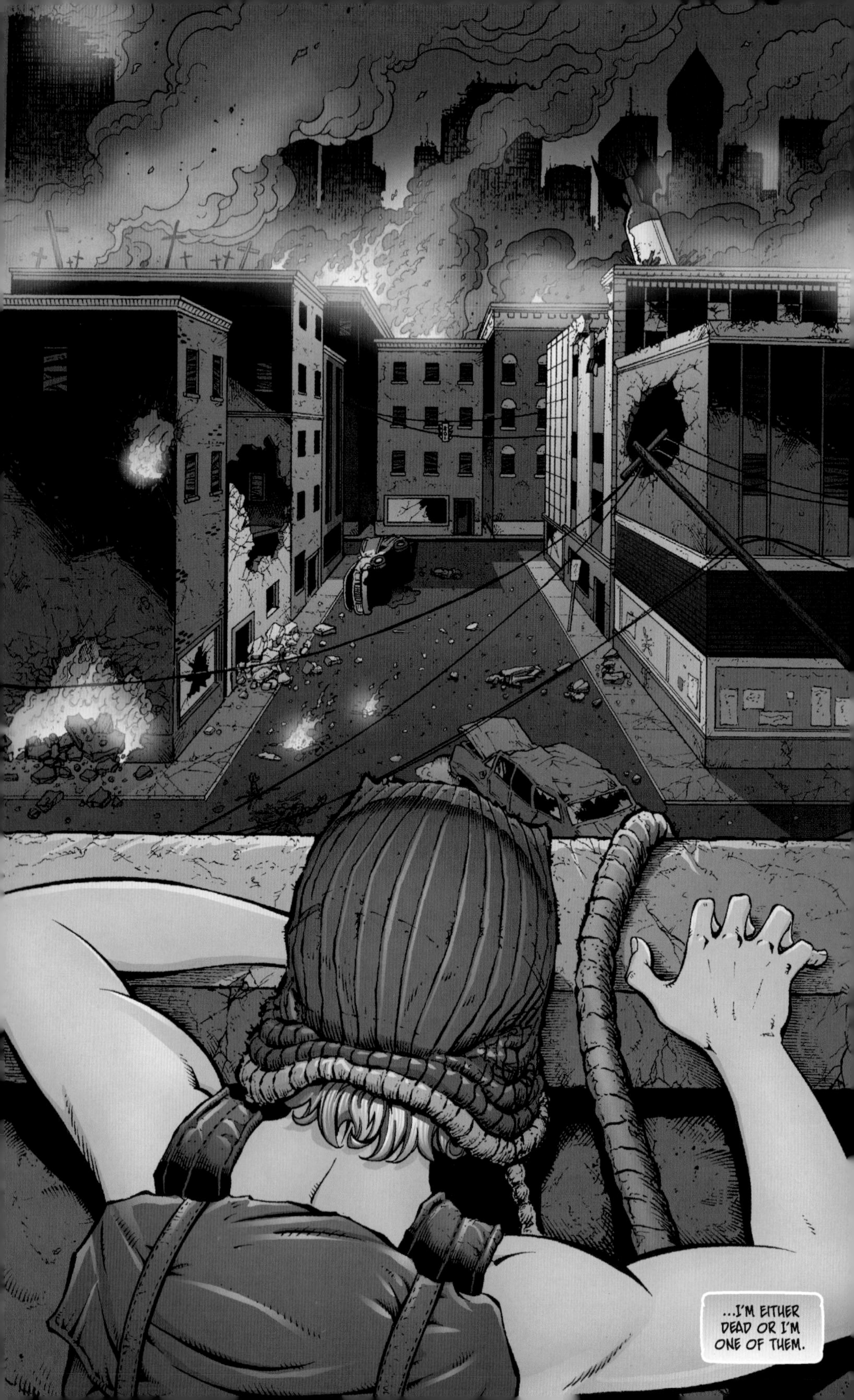
...I'M EITHER
DEAD OR I'M
ONE OF THEM.

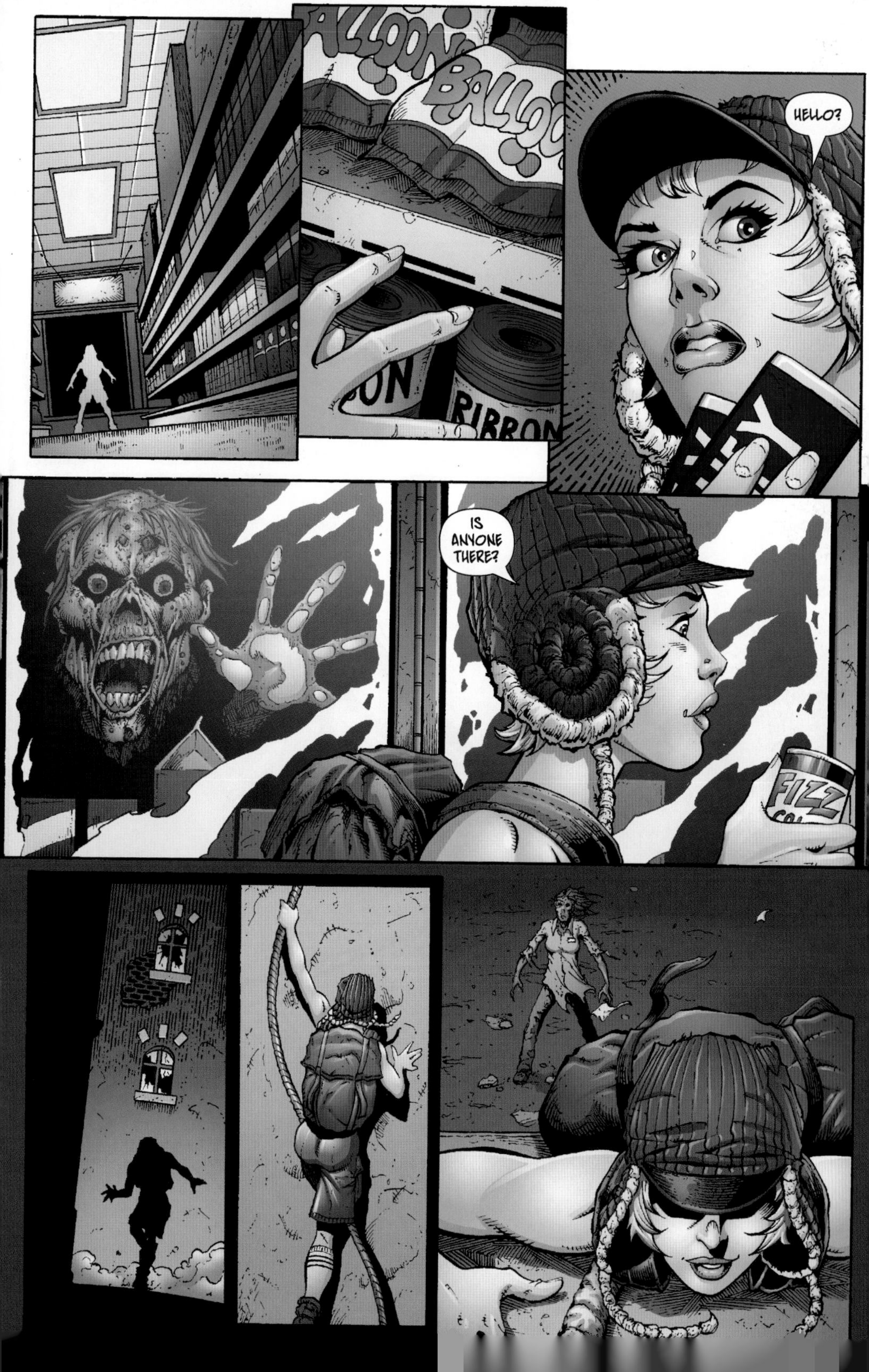
BALLOON
BALLOO
ON
RIBBON
HELLO?
IS ANYONE THERE?
FIZZ

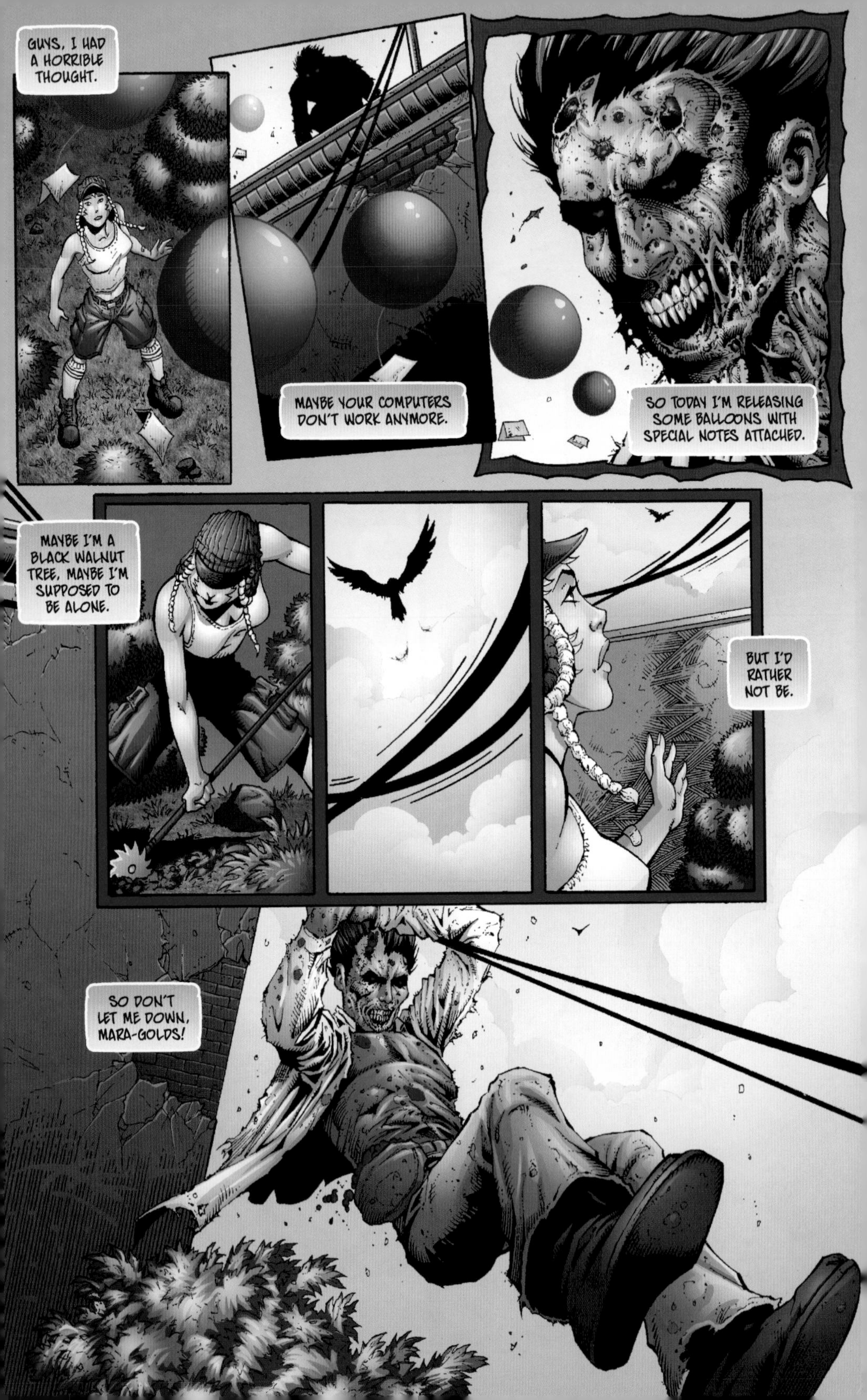
GUYS, I HAD A HORRIBLE THOUGHT.
MAYBE YOUR COMPUTERS DON'T WORK ANYMORE.
SO TODAY I'M RELEASING SOME BALLOONS WITH SPECIAL NOTES ATTACHED.
MAYBE I'M A BLACK WALNUT TREE, MAYBE I'M SUPPOSED TO BE ALONE.
BUT I'D RATHER NOT BE.
SO DON'T LET ME DOWN, MARA-GOLDS!

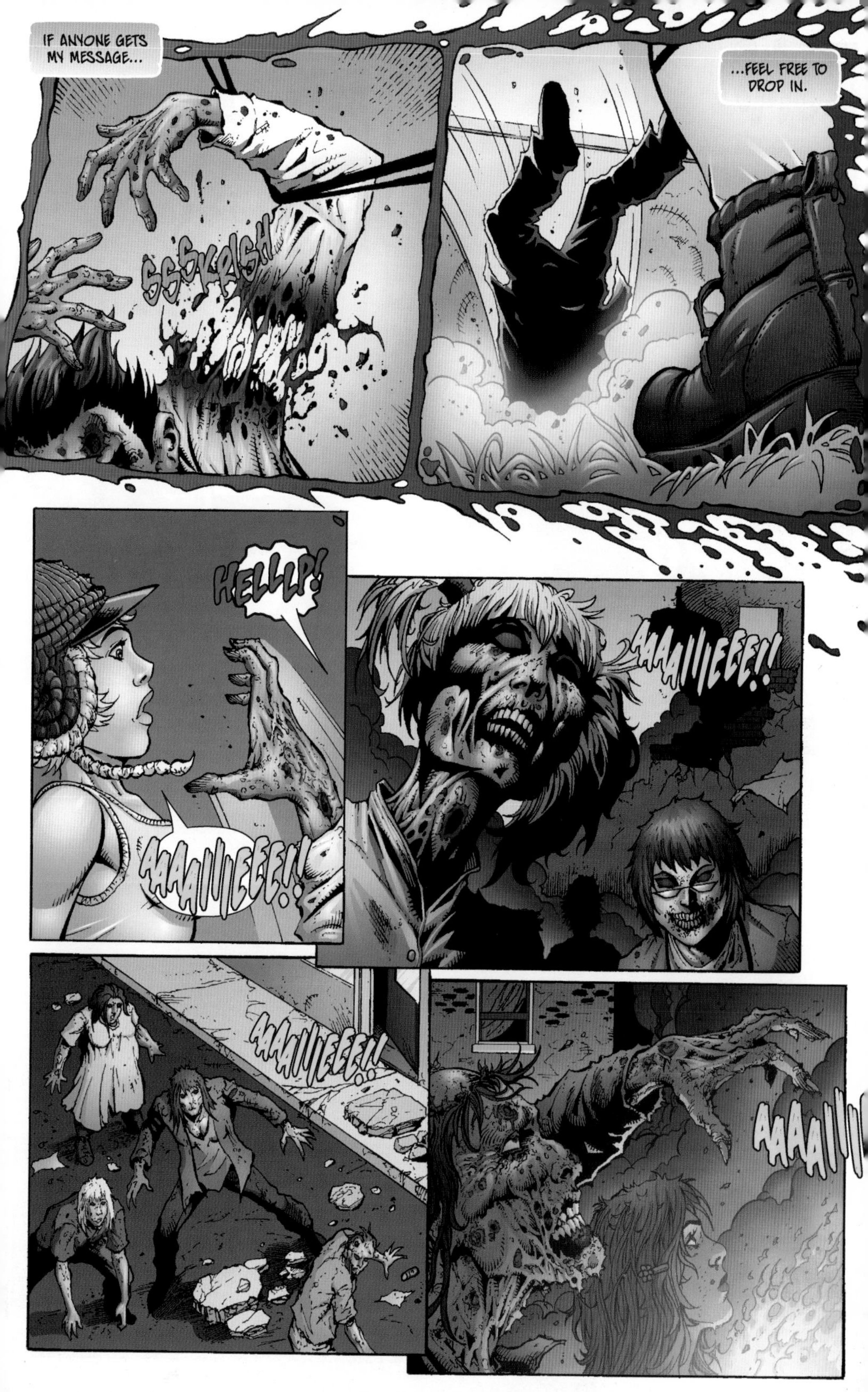
IF ANYONE GETS MY MESSAGE...
SSSKRISH
...FEEL FREE TO DROP IN.
HELLLP!
AAAAIIIEEE!!
AAAAIIIEEE!!
AAAAIIIEEE!!
AAAAIII

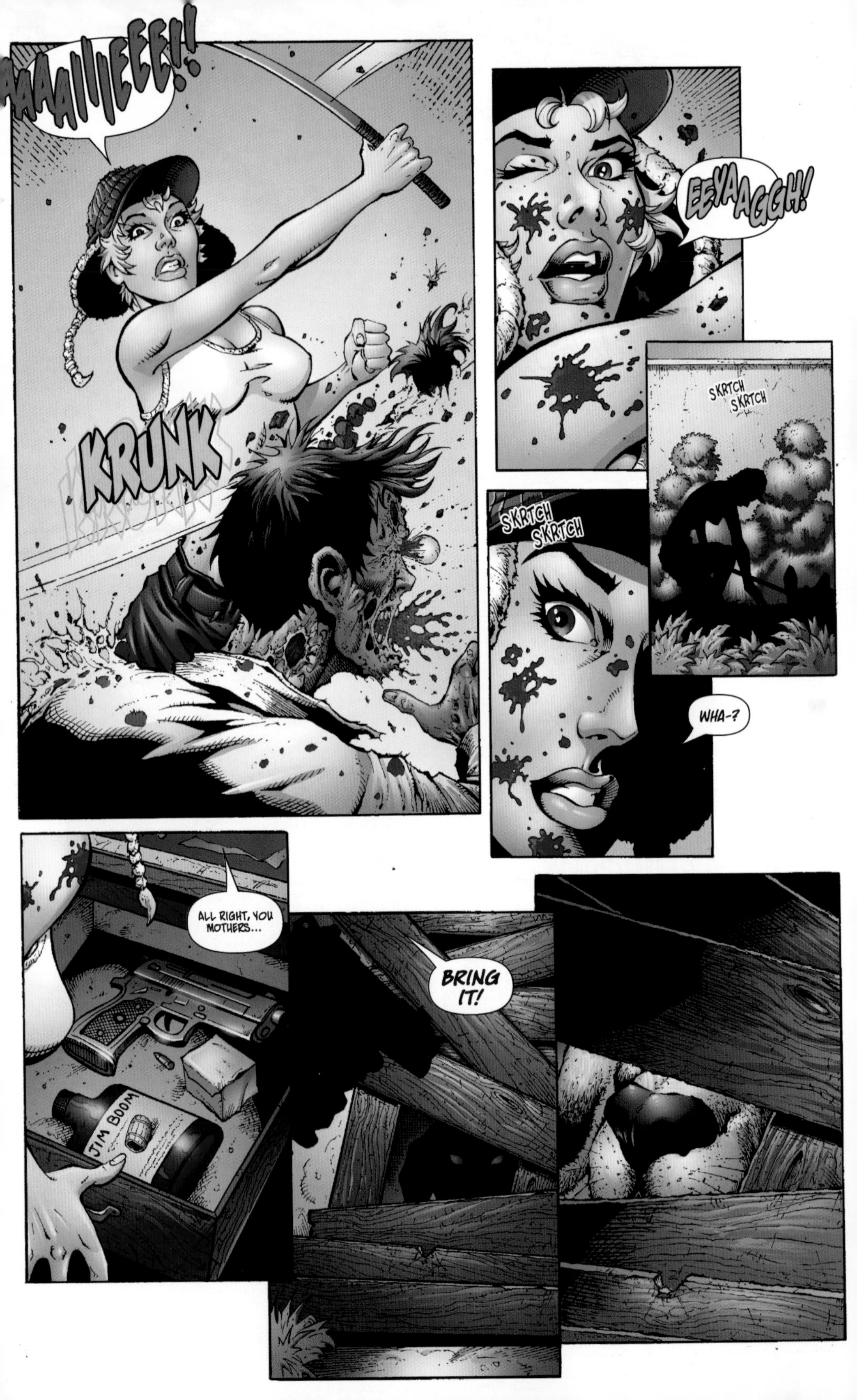
AAAAIIIEEEE!!
KRUNK
EEYAAGGH!
SKRTCH SKRTCH
SKRTCH SKRTCH
WHA-?
ALL RIGHT, YOU MOTHERS...
JIM BOOM
BRING IT!

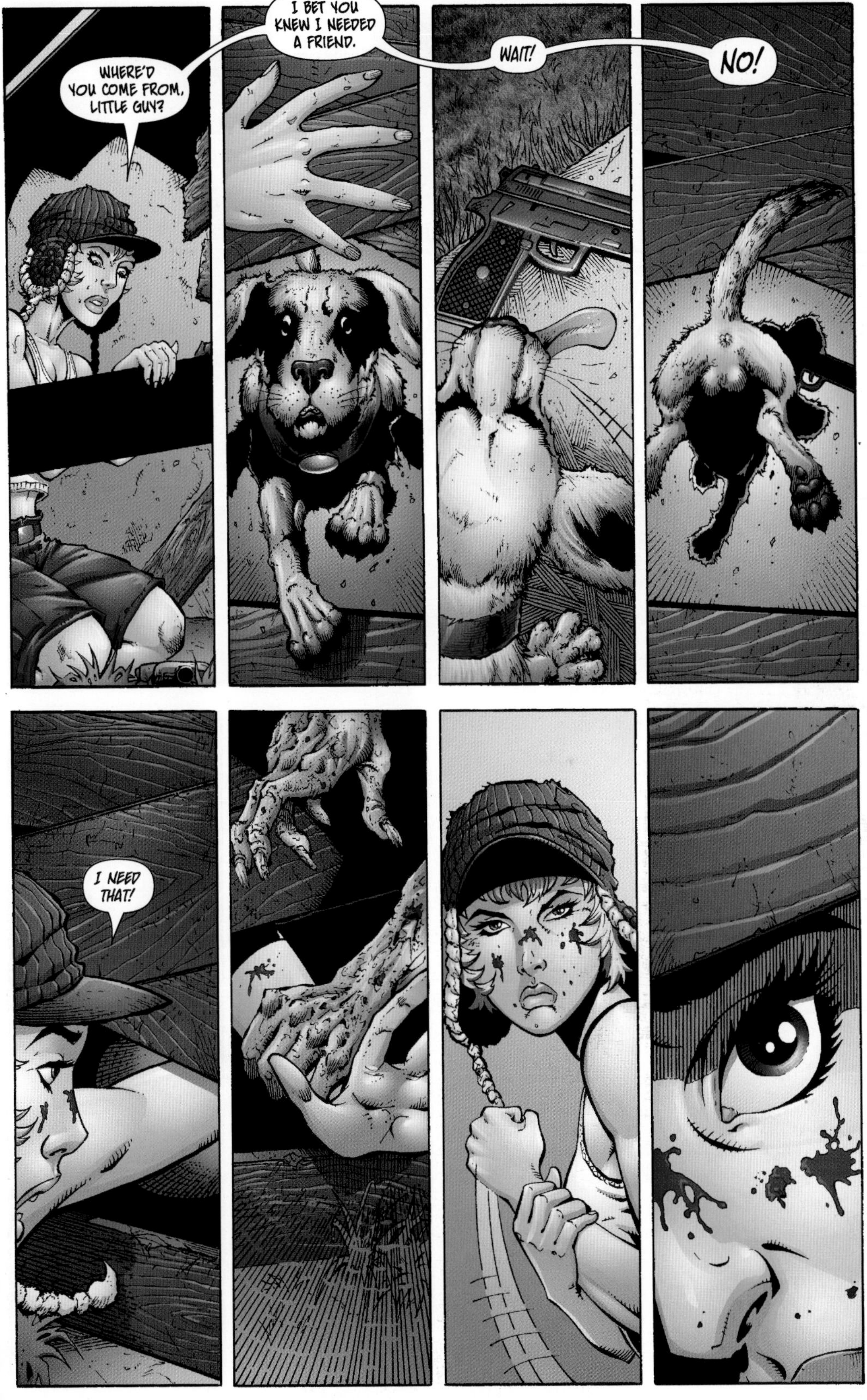
WHERE'D YOU COME FROM, LITTLE GUY?
I BET YOU KNEW I NEEDED A FRIEND.
WAIT!
NO!
I NEED THAT!

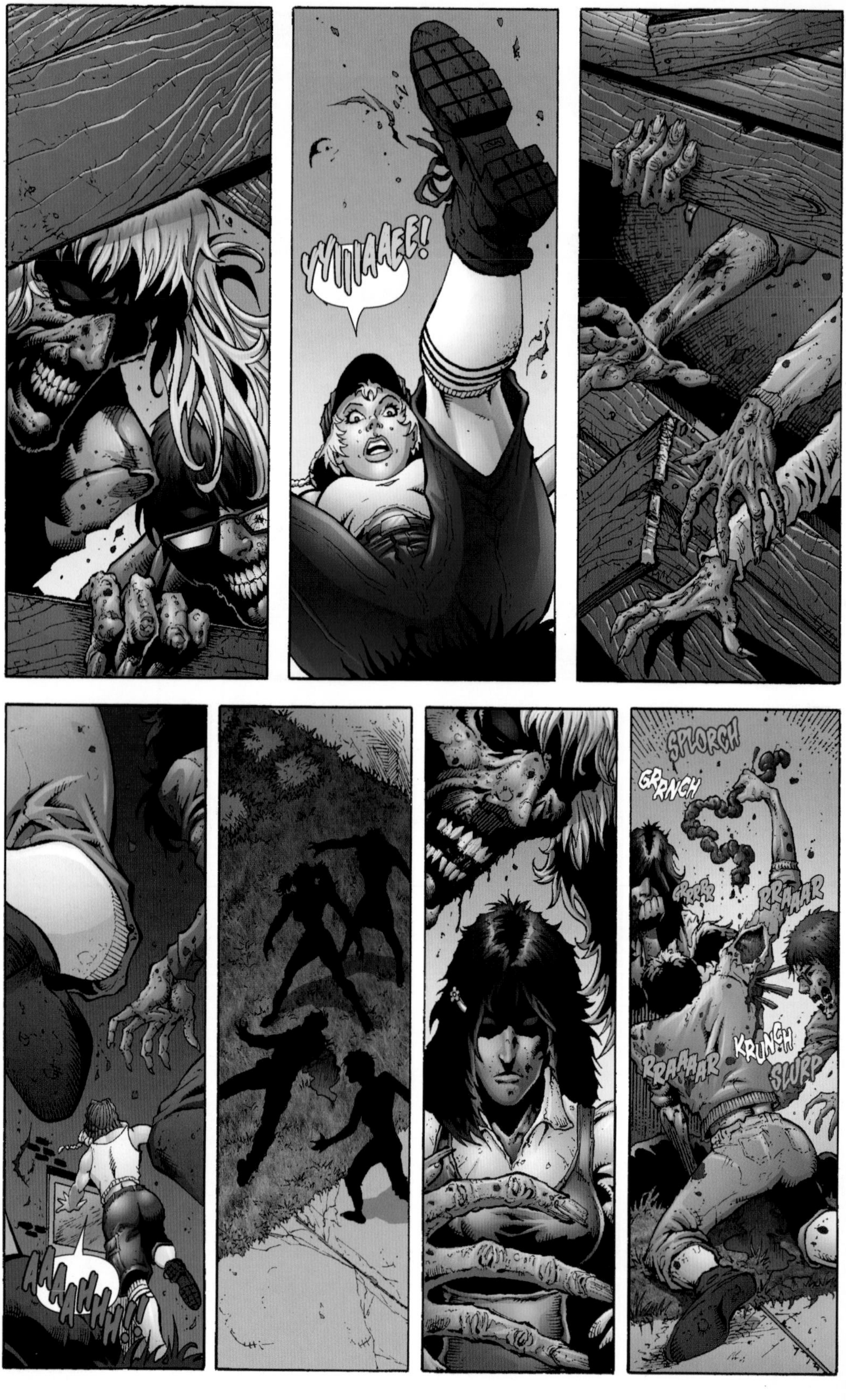
YYIIIIAAEE!
SPLORCH
GRRNCH
GRRRR
RRAAAR
KRUNCH
RRAAAAR
SLURP
AAAAHHH!!

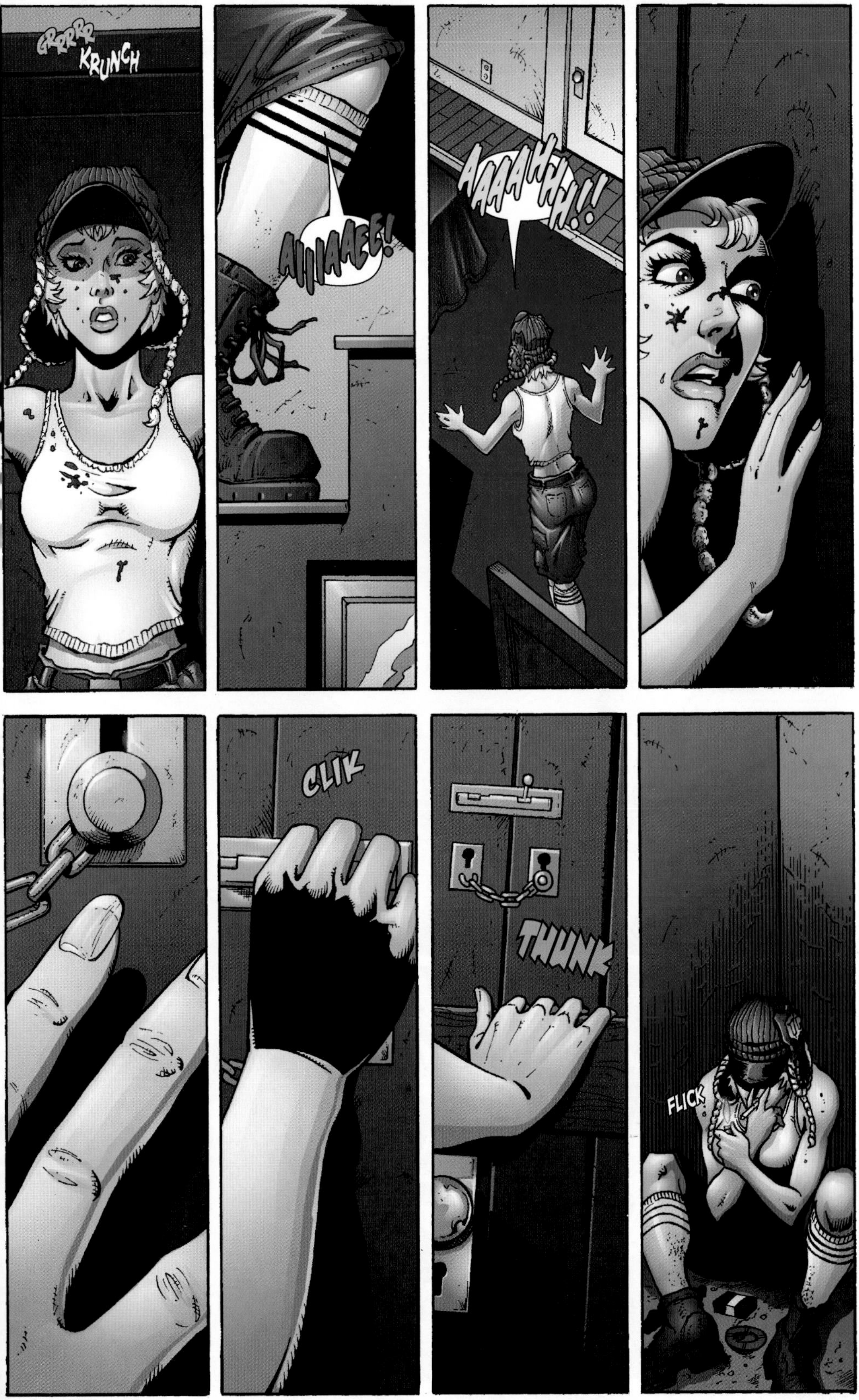
GRRRRR
KRUNCH
AIIIAAEE!
AAAAHHHH!!
CLIK
THUNK
FLICK

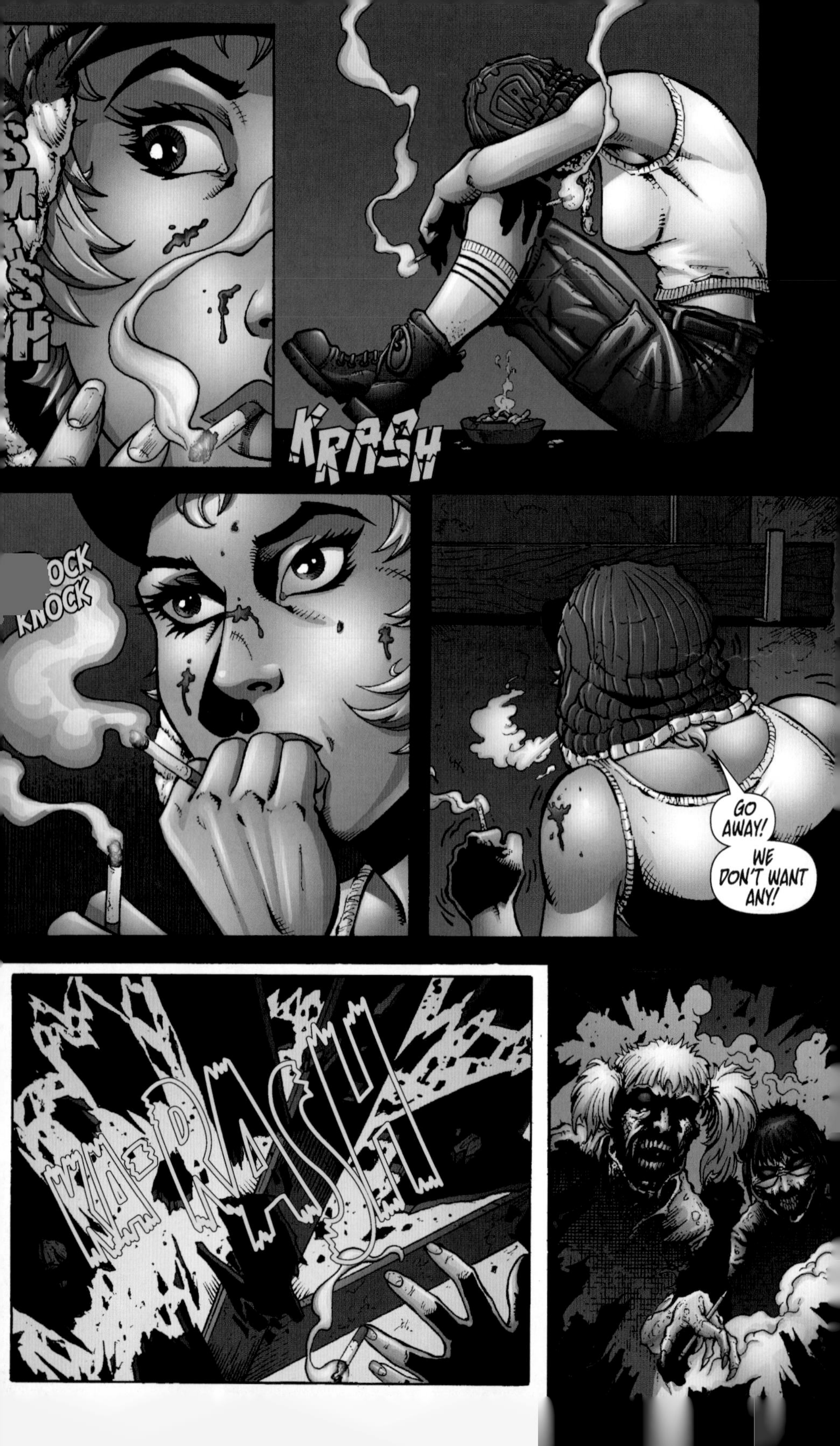
KRASH
KNOCK
GO AWAY!
WE DON'T WANT ANY!
KABRASH

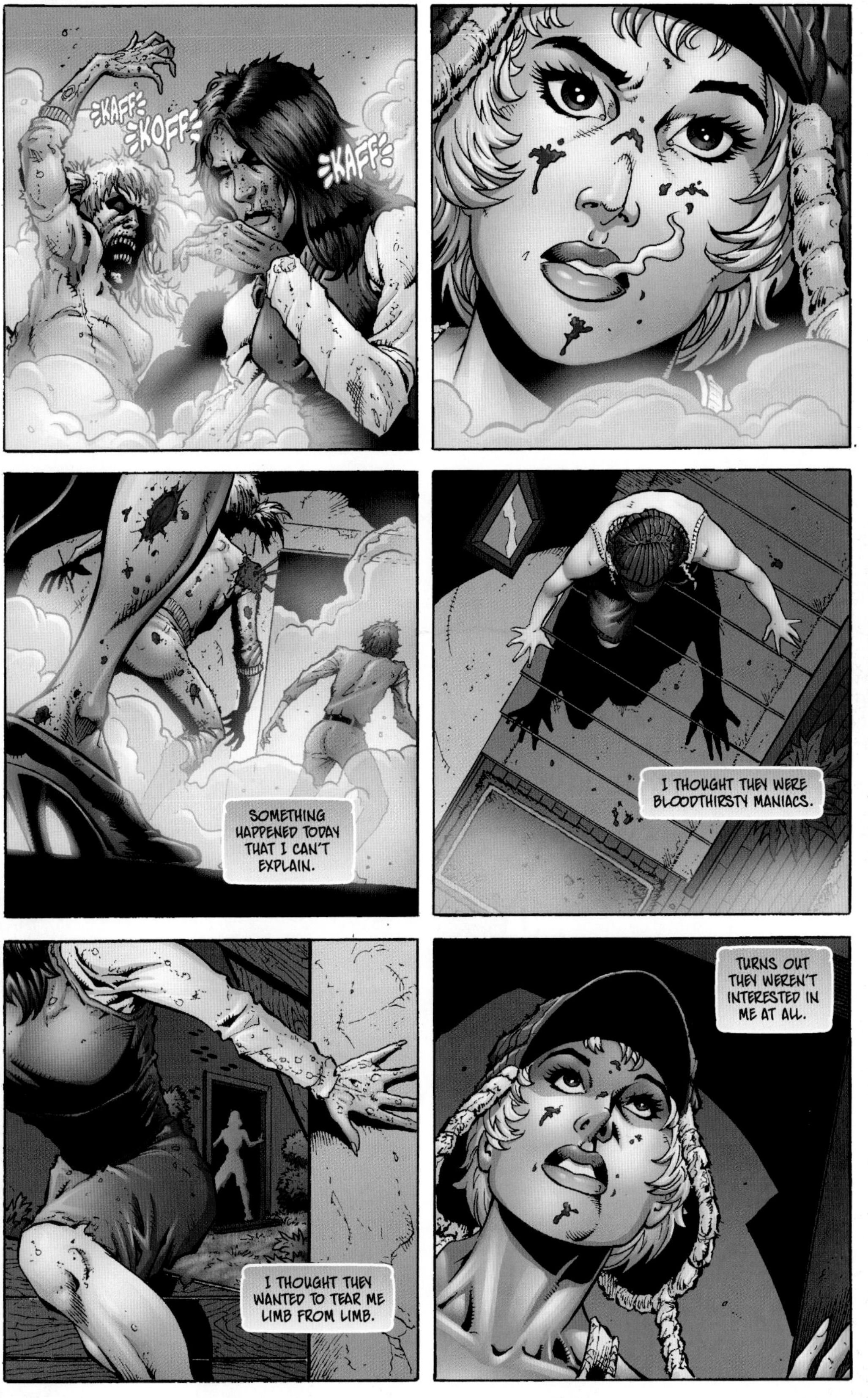
KAFF
KOFF
KAFF
SOMETHING HAPPENED TODAY THAT I CAN'T EXPLAIN.
I THOUGHT THEY WERE BLOODTHIRSTY MANIACS.
I THOUGHT THEY WANTED TO TEAR ME LIMB FROM LIMB.
TURNS OUT THEY WEREN'T INTERESTED IN ME AT ALL.

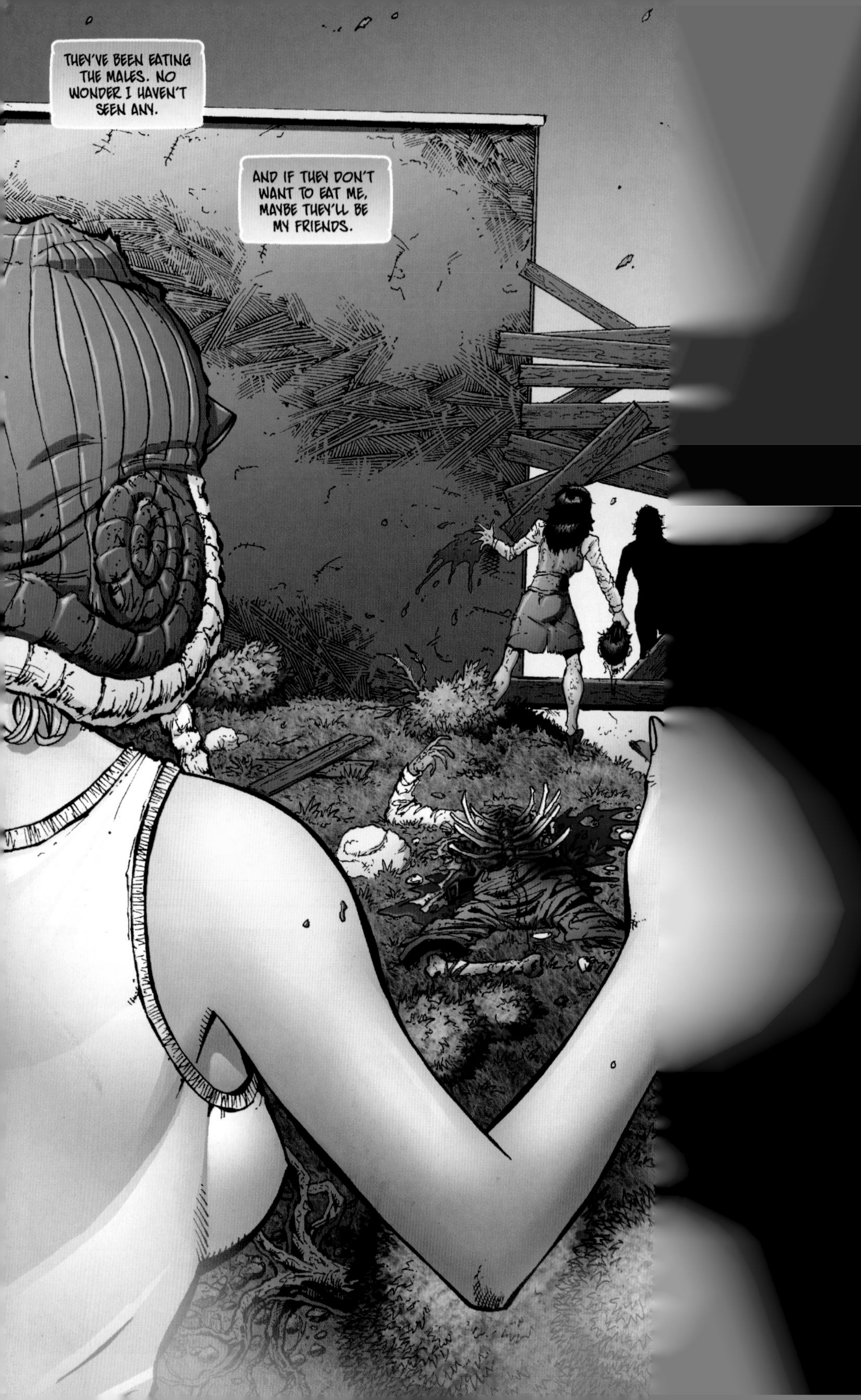
THEY'VE BEEN EATING THE MALES. NO WONDER I HAVEN'T SEEN ANY.
AND IF THEY DON'T WANT TO EAT ME, MAYBE THEY'LL BE MY FRIENDS.

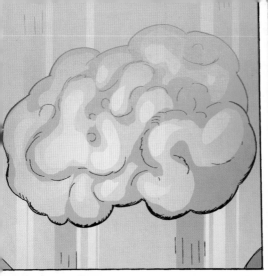

OKAY, MARA-GOLDS, THERE'S JUST ONE RULE WHEN MAKING FRIENDS. "BAKED GOODS ARE BEST."

AND ANOTHER RULE IS "DRESS TO IMPRESS."

AND THE FINAL RULE IS "EVERYTHING'S BETTER IN A BASKET."

THEY WON'T KNOW WHAT HIT THEIR TASTE BUDS. IF THEY STILL HAVE THEM.

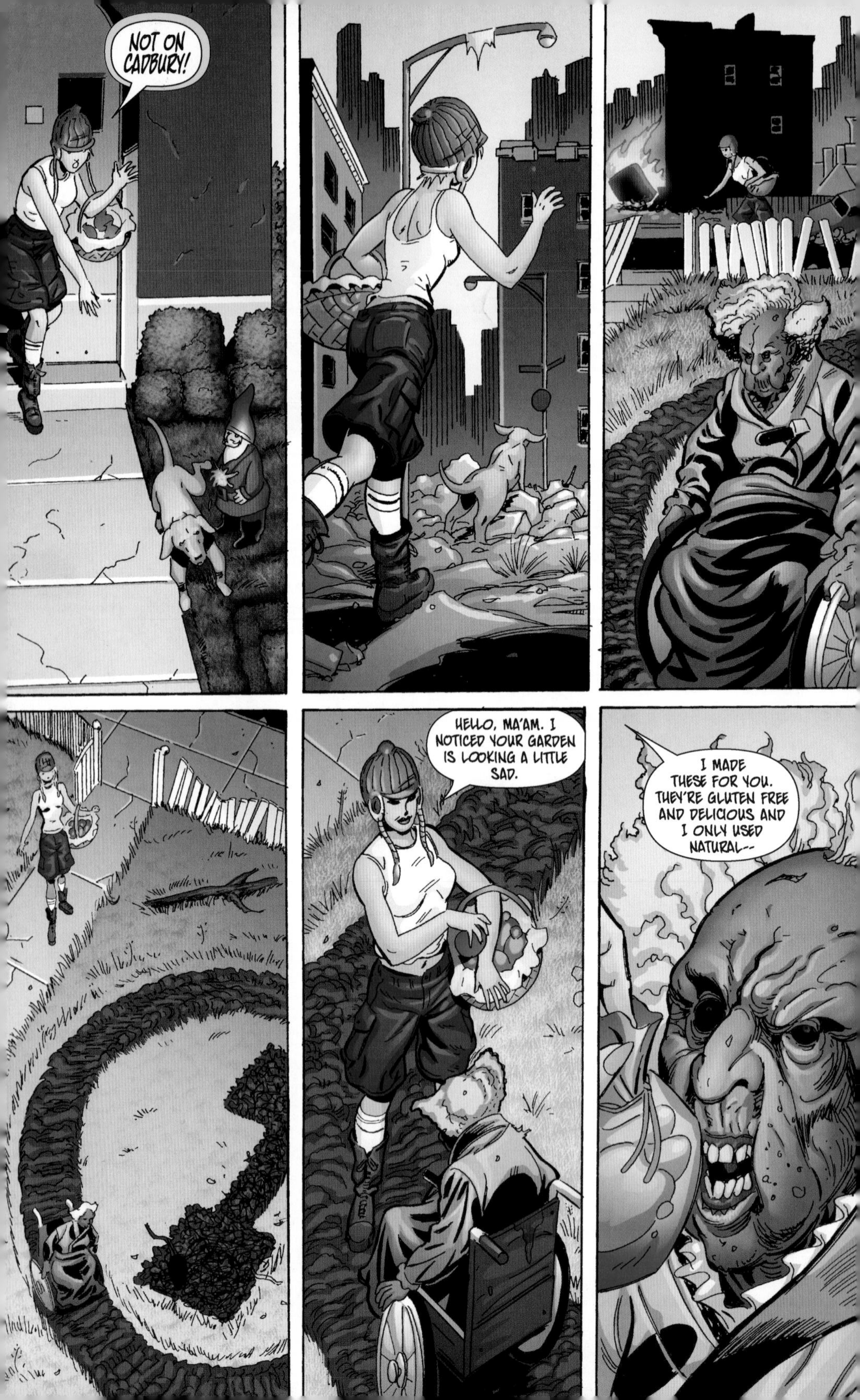
NOT ON CADBURY!
HELLO, MA'AM. I NOTICED YOUR GARDEN IS LOOKING A LITTLE SAD.
I MADE THESE FOR YOU. THEY'RE GLUTEN FREE AND DELICIOUS AND I ONLY USED NATURAL--

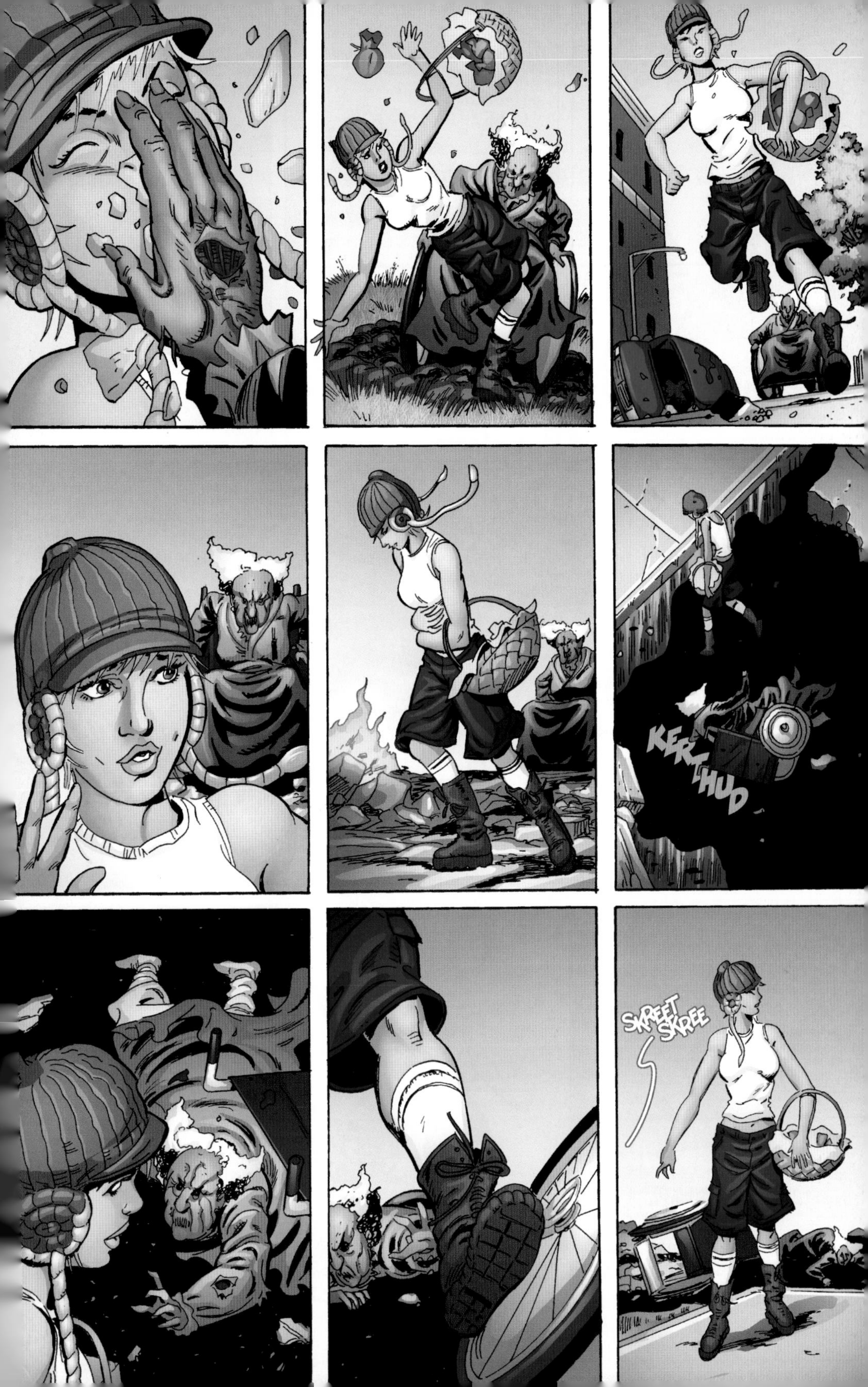
KERTHUD
SKREET SKREE

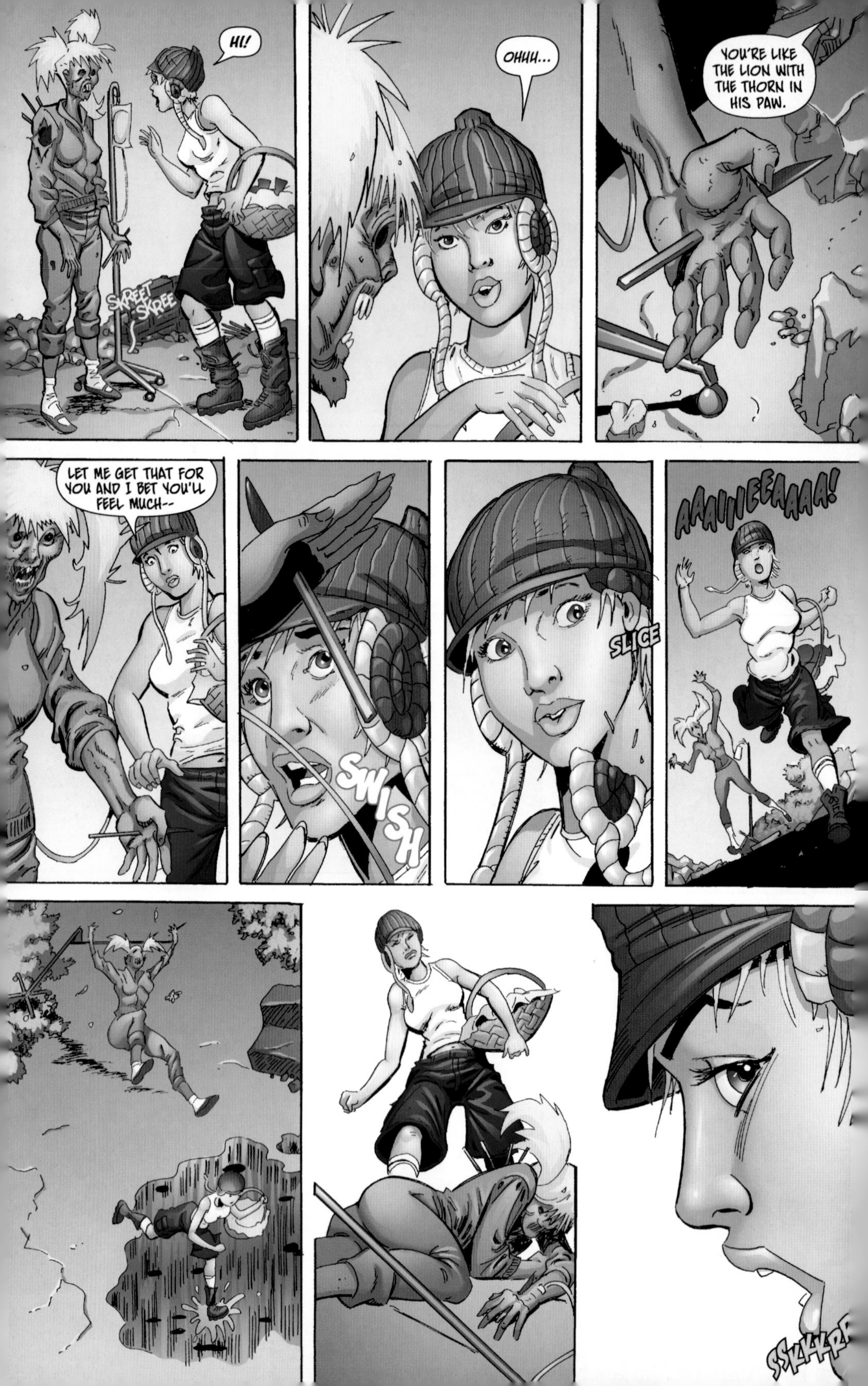
HI!
SKREET SKREE
OHHU...
YOU'RE LIKE THE LION WITH THE THORN IN HIS PAW.
LET ME GET THAT FOR YOU AND I BET YOU'LL FEEL MUCH--
SWISH
SLICE
AAAIIIEEAAAA!

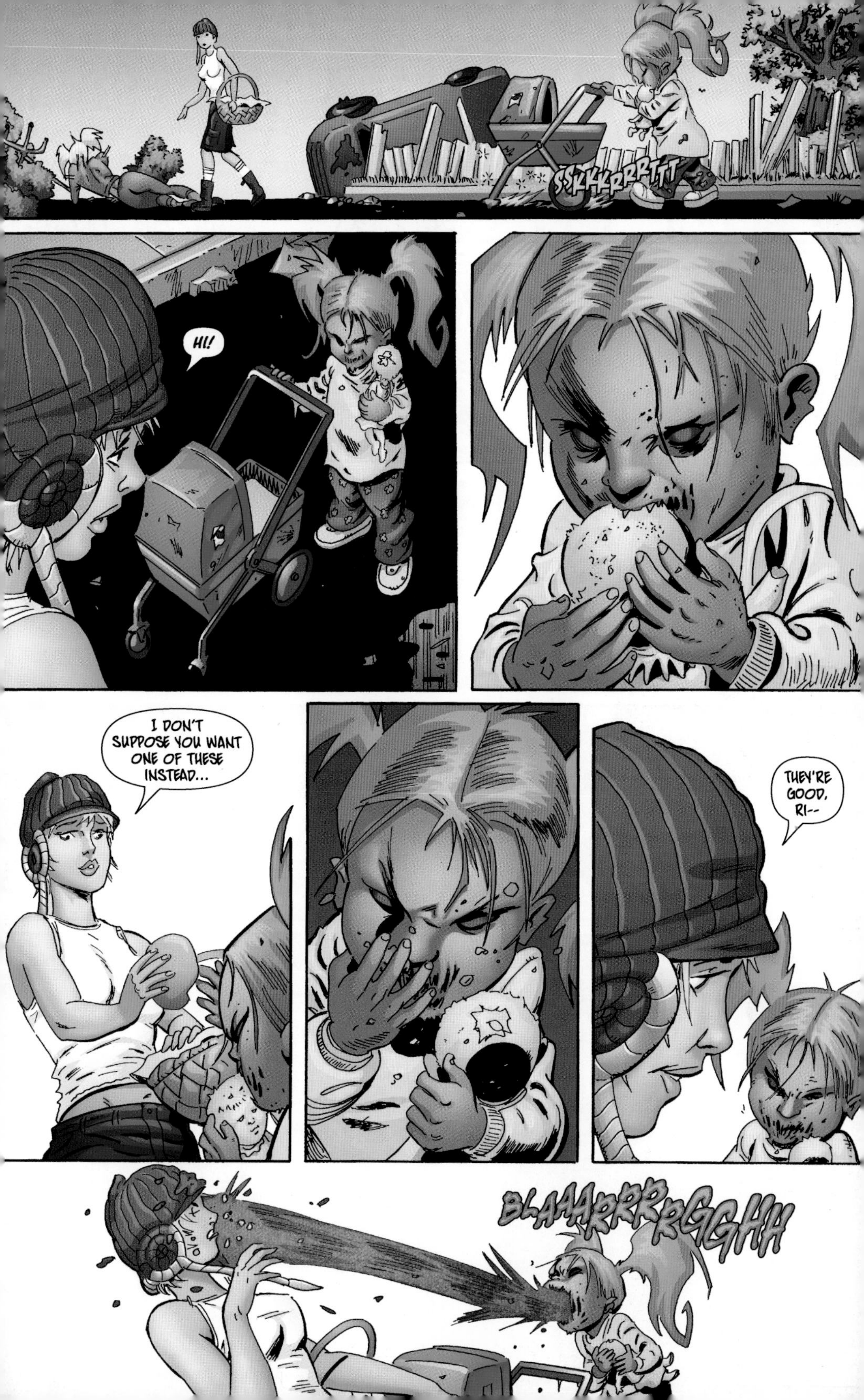
SSKKKRRRTTT
HI!
I DON'T SUPPOSE YOU WANT ONE OF THESE INSTEAD...
THEY'RE GOOD, RI--
BLAAARRRRGGHH

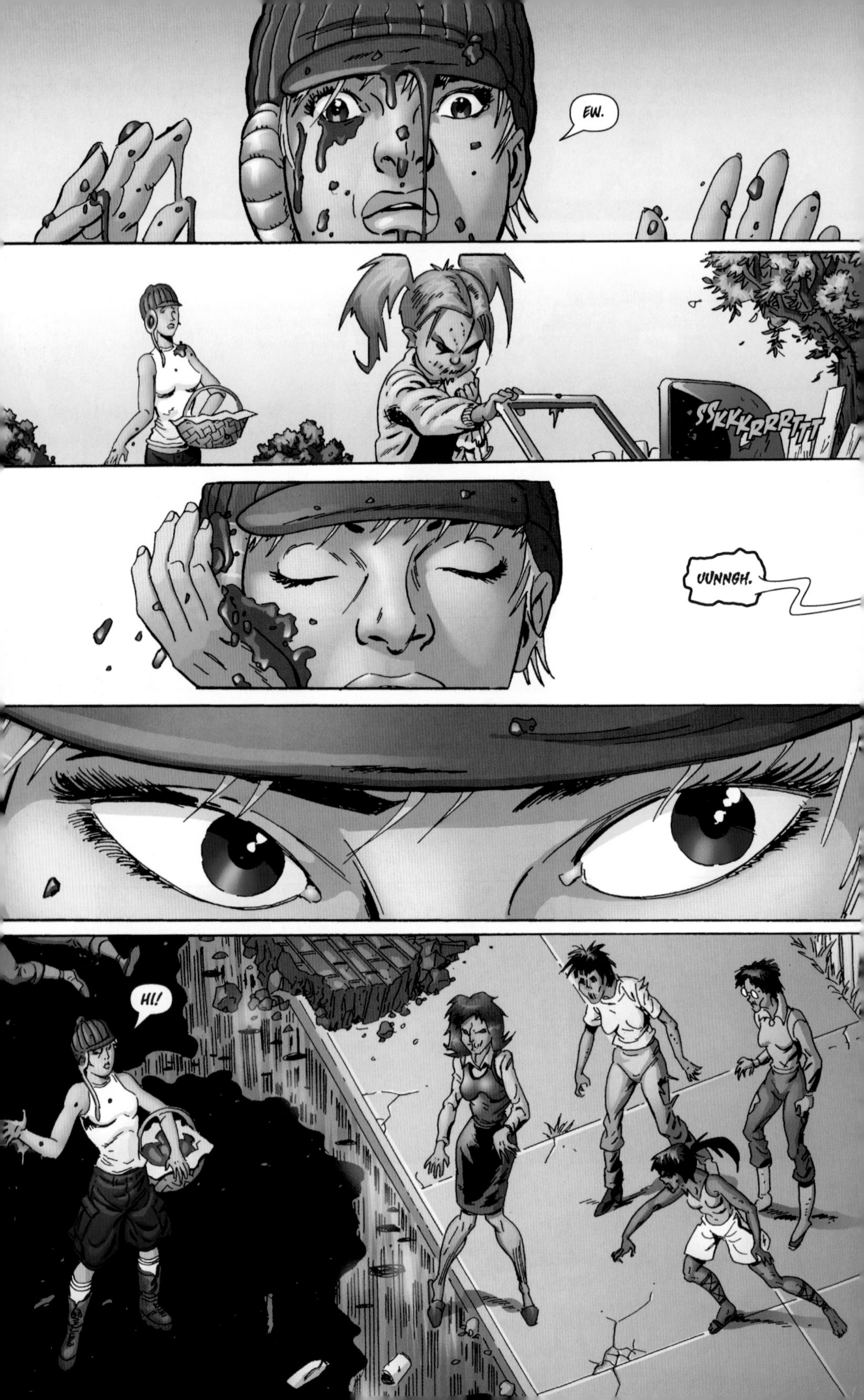
EW.
SSKKKLRRRTTT
UUNNGH.
HI!

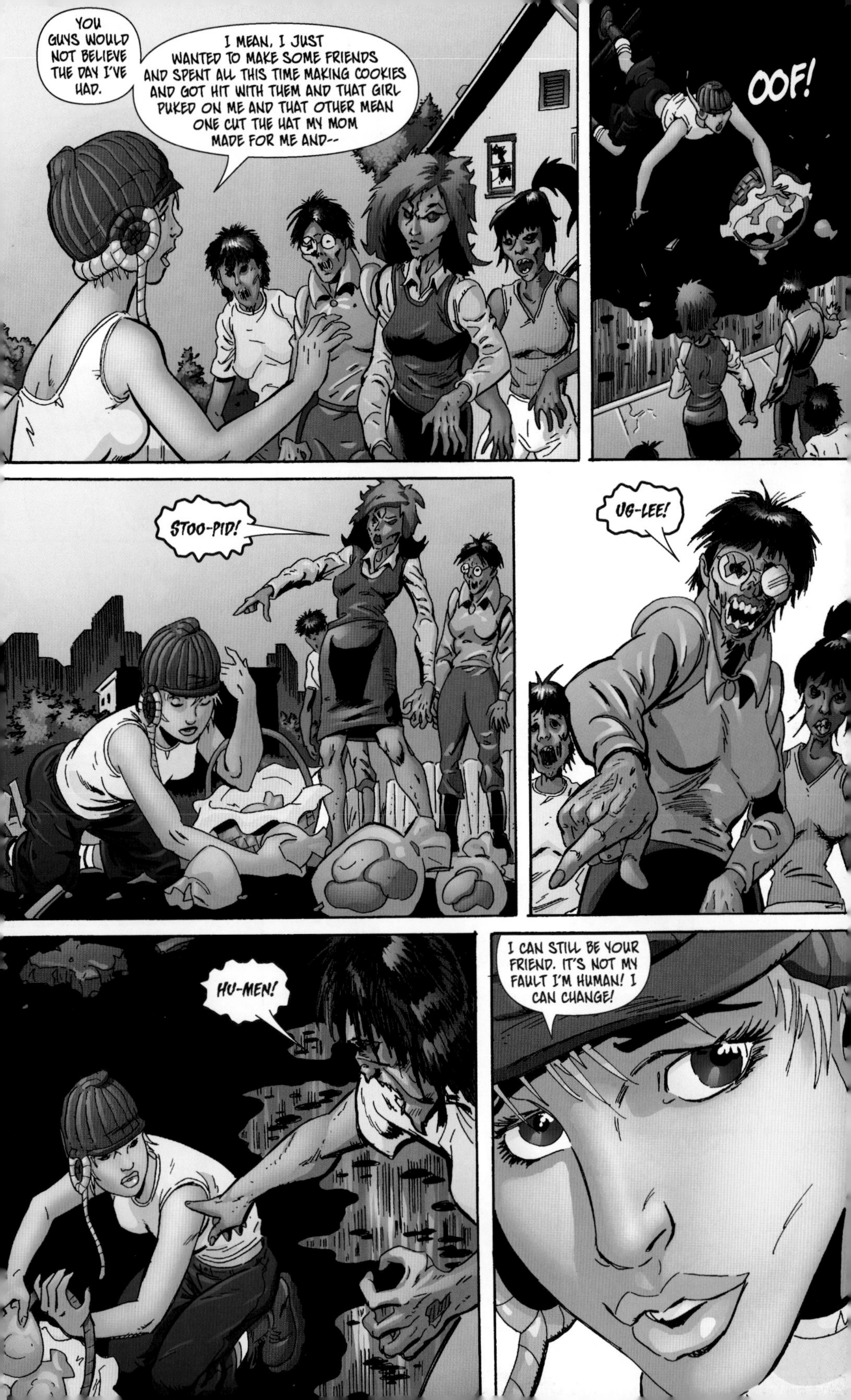
YOU GUYS WOULD NOT BELIEVE THE DAY I'VE HAD.
I MEAN, I JUST WANTED TO MAKE SOME FRIENDS AND SPENT ALL THIS TIME MAKING COOKIES AND GOT HIT WITH THEM AND THAT GIRL PUKED ON ME AND THAT OTHER MEAN ONE CUT THE HAT MY MOM MADE FOR ME AND--
OOF!
STOO-PID!
UG-LEE!
HU-MEN!
I CAN STILL BE YOUR FRIEND. IT'S NOT MY FAULT I'M HUMAN! I CAN CHANGE!

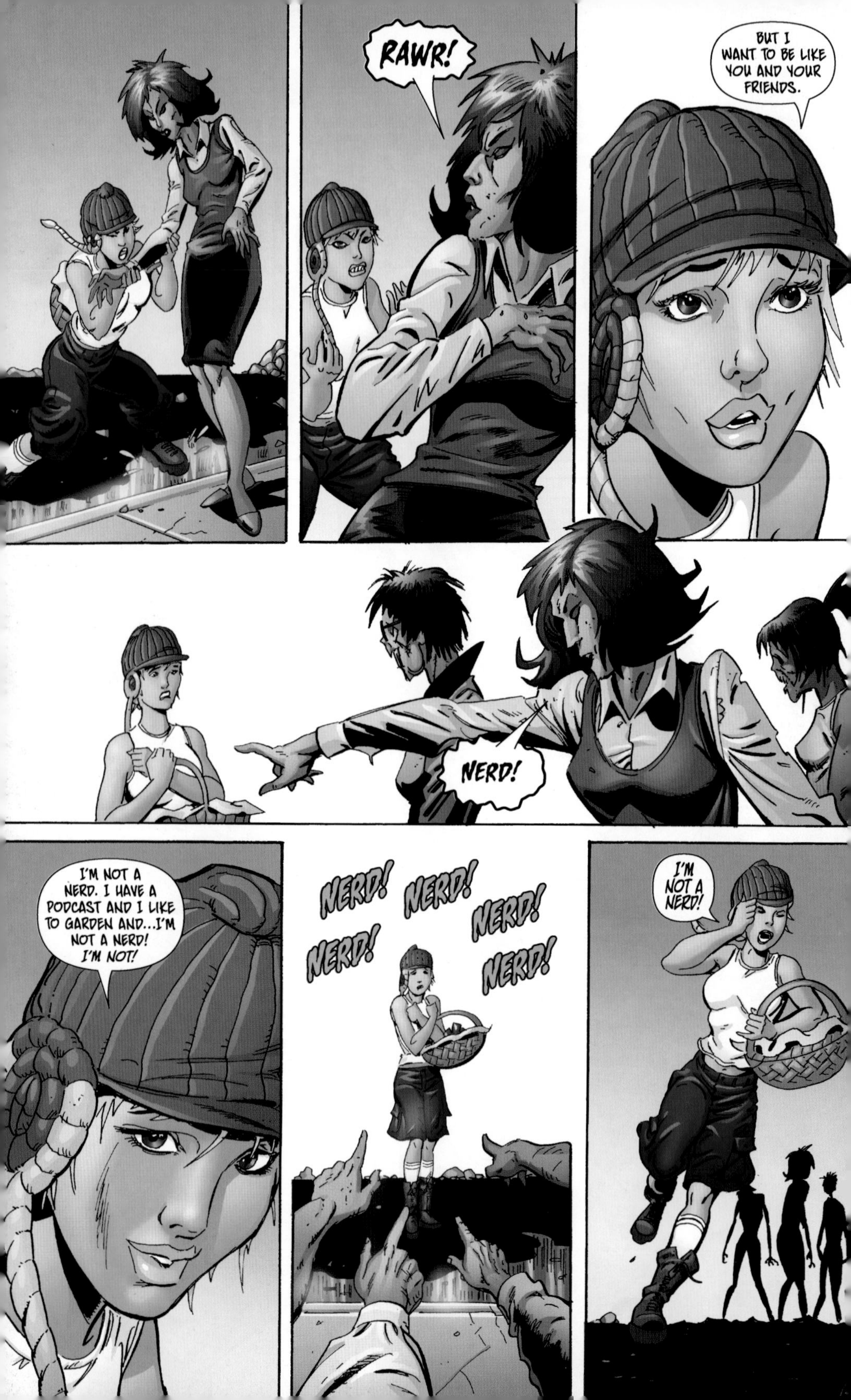
RAWR!
BUT I WANT TO BE LIKE YOU AND YOUR FRIENDS.
NERD!
I'M NOT A NERD. I HAVE A PODCAST AND I LIKE TO GARDEN AND...I'M NOT A NERD! I'M NOT!
NERD!
NERD!
NERD!
NERD!
NERD!
I'M NOT A NERD!

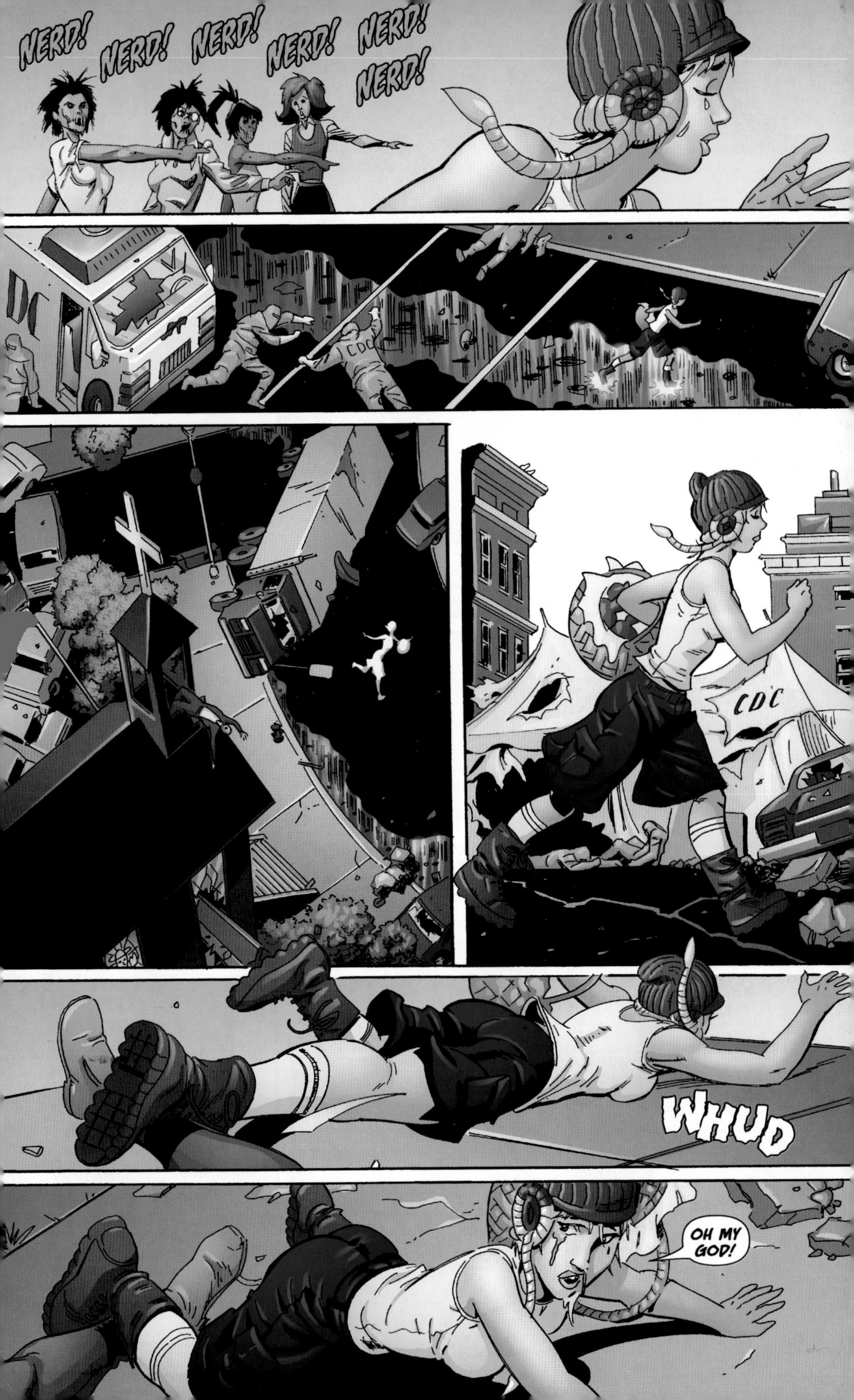
NERD!
NERD!
NERD!
NERD!
NERD!
NERD!
CDC
CDC
WHUD
OH MY GOD!

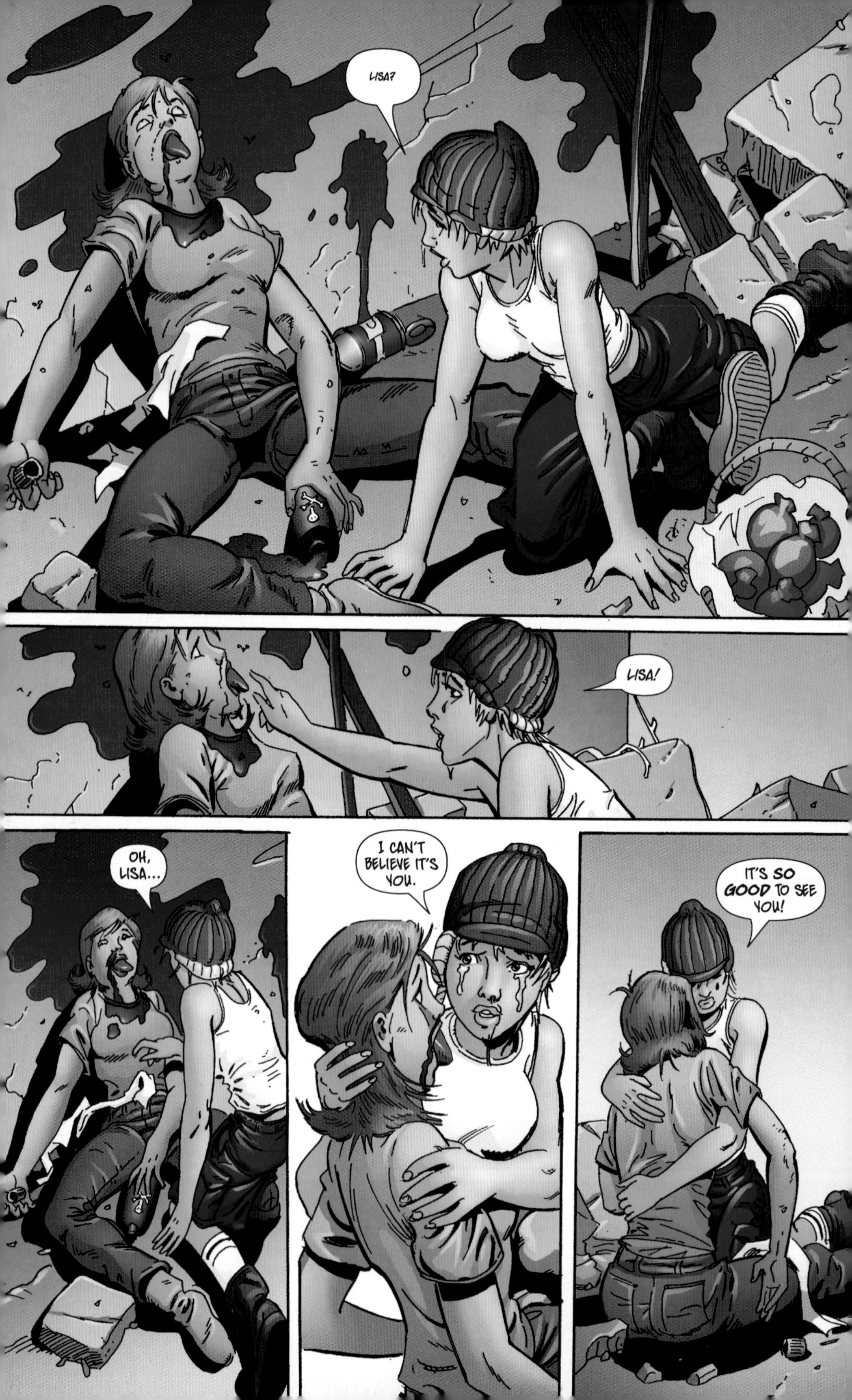
LISA?
LISA!
OH, LISA...
I CAN'T BELIEVE IT'S YOU.
IT'S SO GOOD TO SEE YOU!

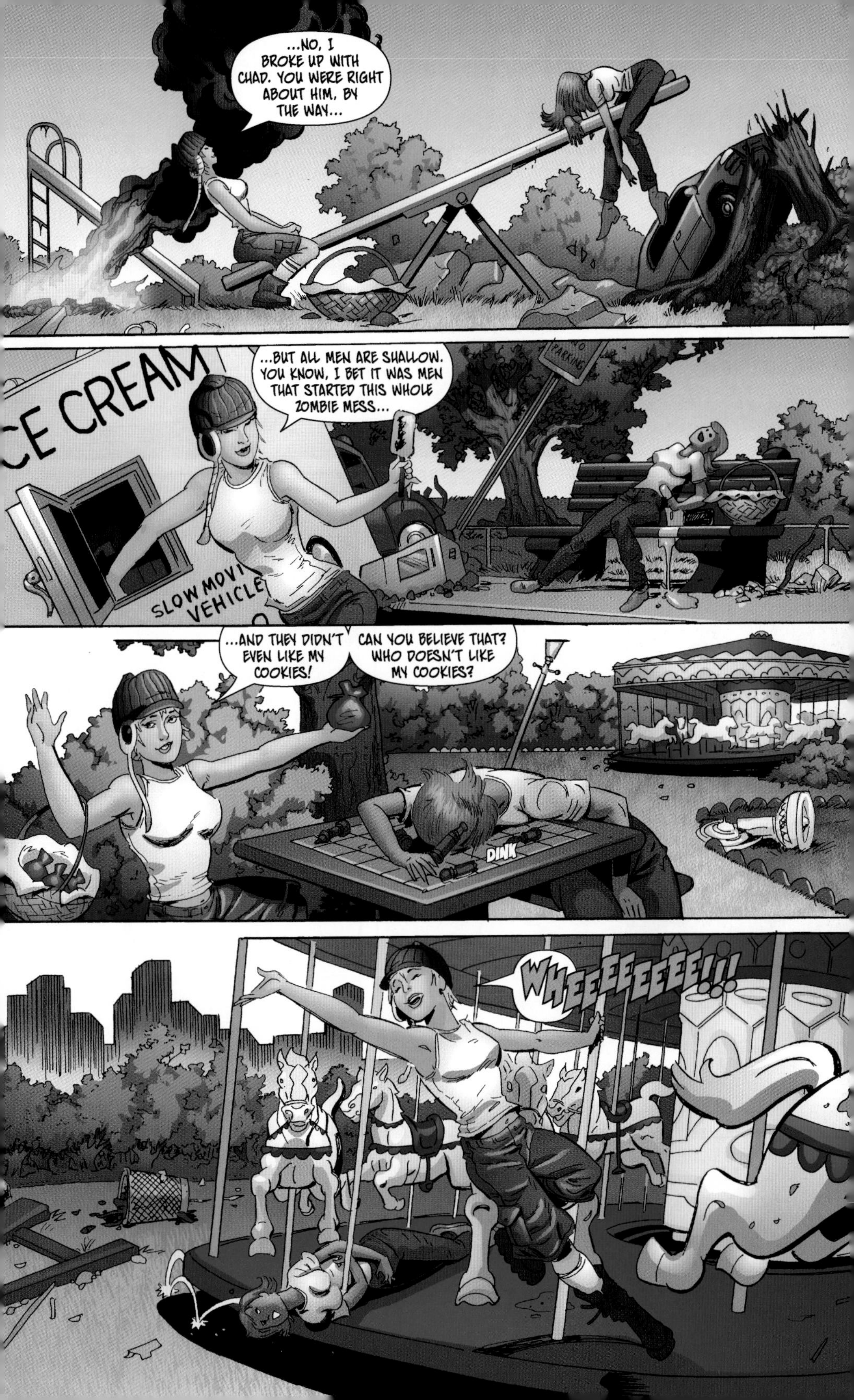
...NO, I BROKE UP WITH CHAD. YOU WERE RIGHT ABOUT HIM, BY THE WAY...
...BUT ALL MEN ARE SHALLOW. YOU KNOW, I BET IT WAS MEN THAT STARTED THIS WHOLE ZOMBIE MESS...
CE CREAM
SLOW MOVI
VEHICLE
NO PARKING
...AND THEY DIDN'T EVEN LIKE MY COOKIES!
CAN YOU BELIEVE THAT? WHO DOESN'T LIKE MY COOKIES?
DINK
WHEEEEEEEE!!!

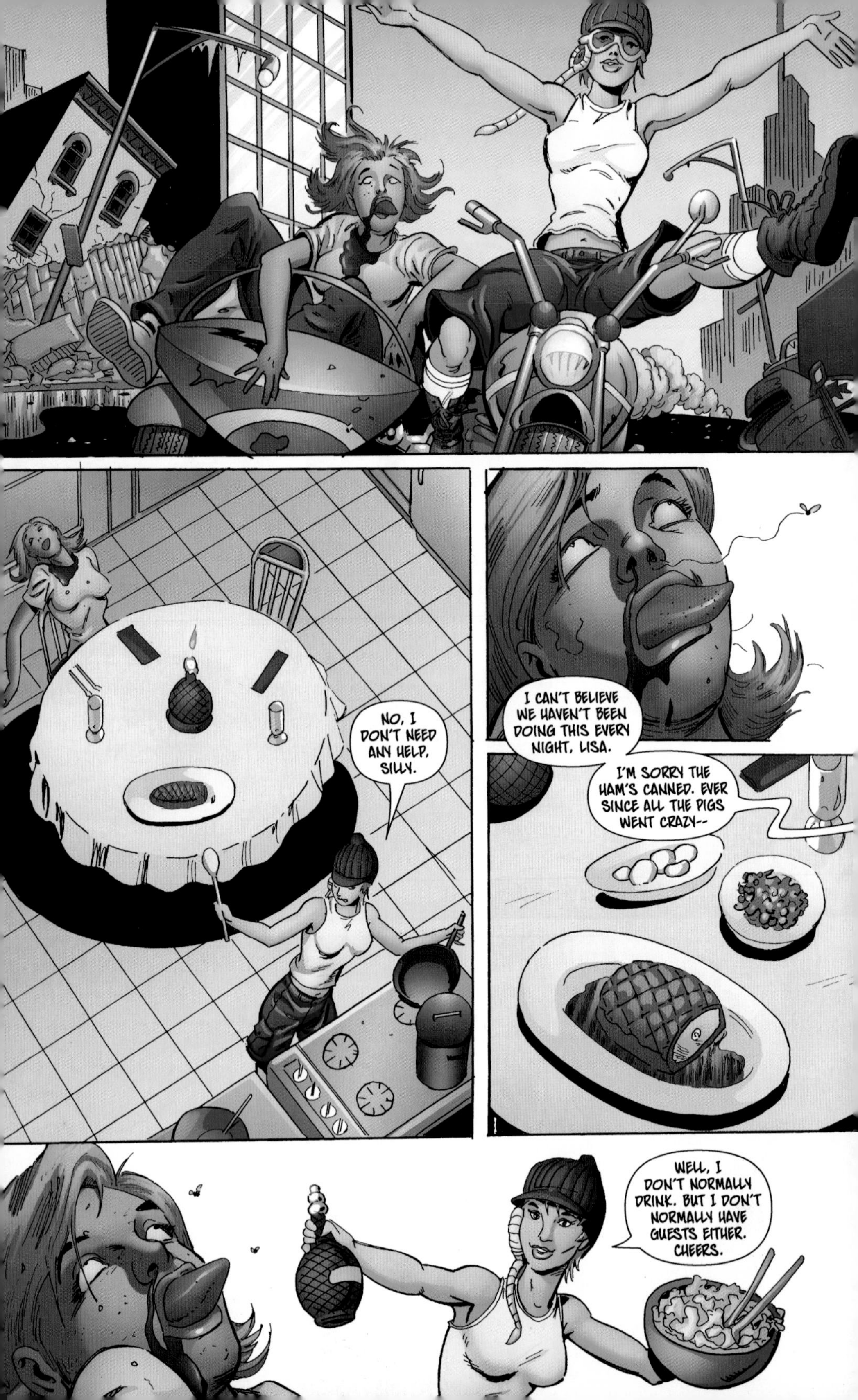
NO, I DON'T NEED ANY HELP, SILLY.
I CAN'T BELIEVE WE HAVEN'T BEEN DOING THIS EVERY NIGHT, LISA.
I'M SORRY THE HAM'S CANNED. EVER SINCE ALL THE PIGS WENT CRAZY--
WELL, I DON'T NORMALLY DRINK. BUT I DON'T NORMALLY HAVE GUESTS EITHER. CHEERS.

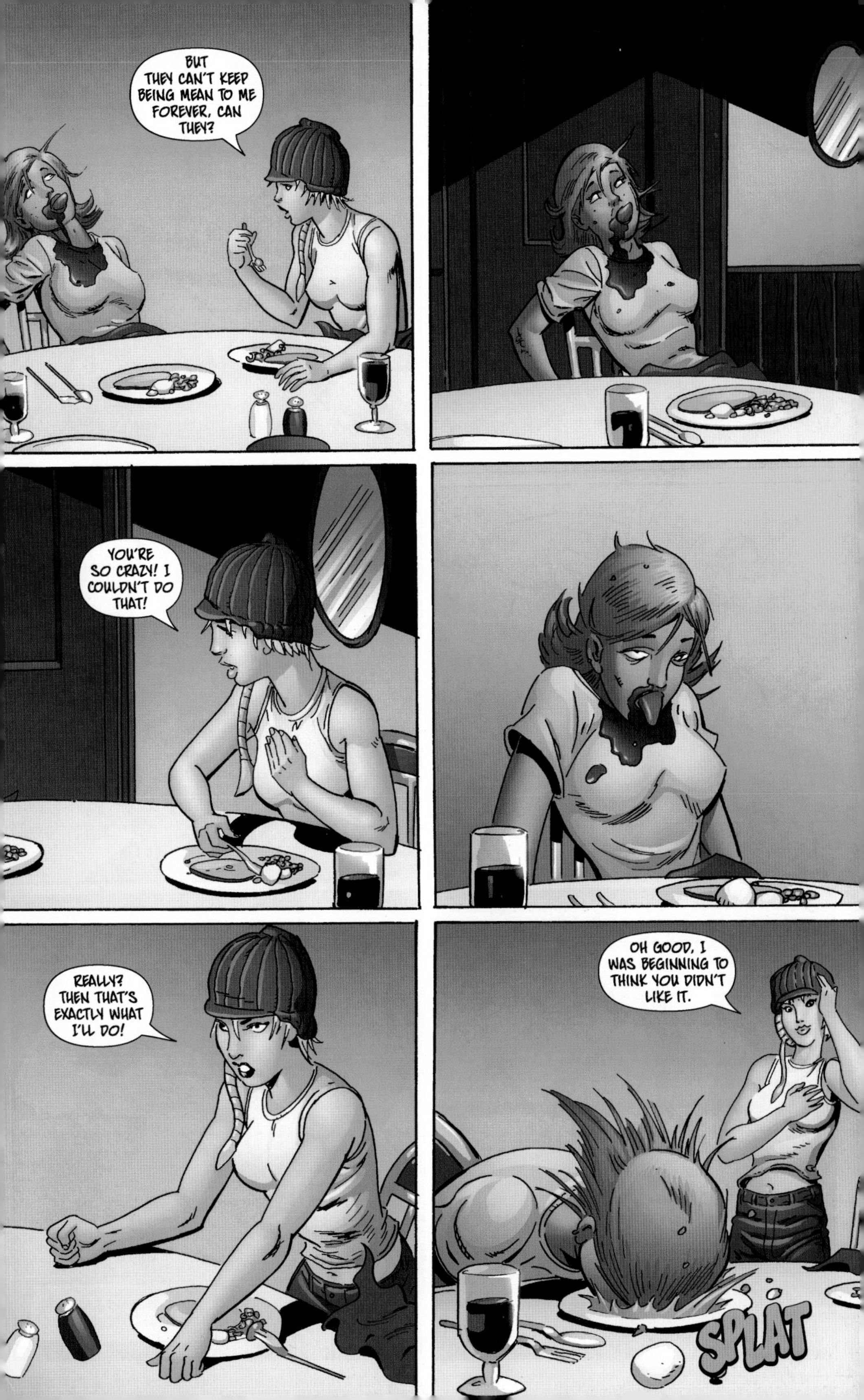
BUT THEY CAN'T KEEP BEING MEAN TO ME FOREVER, CAN THEY?
YOU'RE SO CRAZY! I COULDN'T DO THAT!
REALLY? THEN THAT'S EXACTLY WHAT I'LL DO!
OH GOOD, I WAS BEGINNING TO THINK YOU DIDN'T LIKE IT.
SPLAT

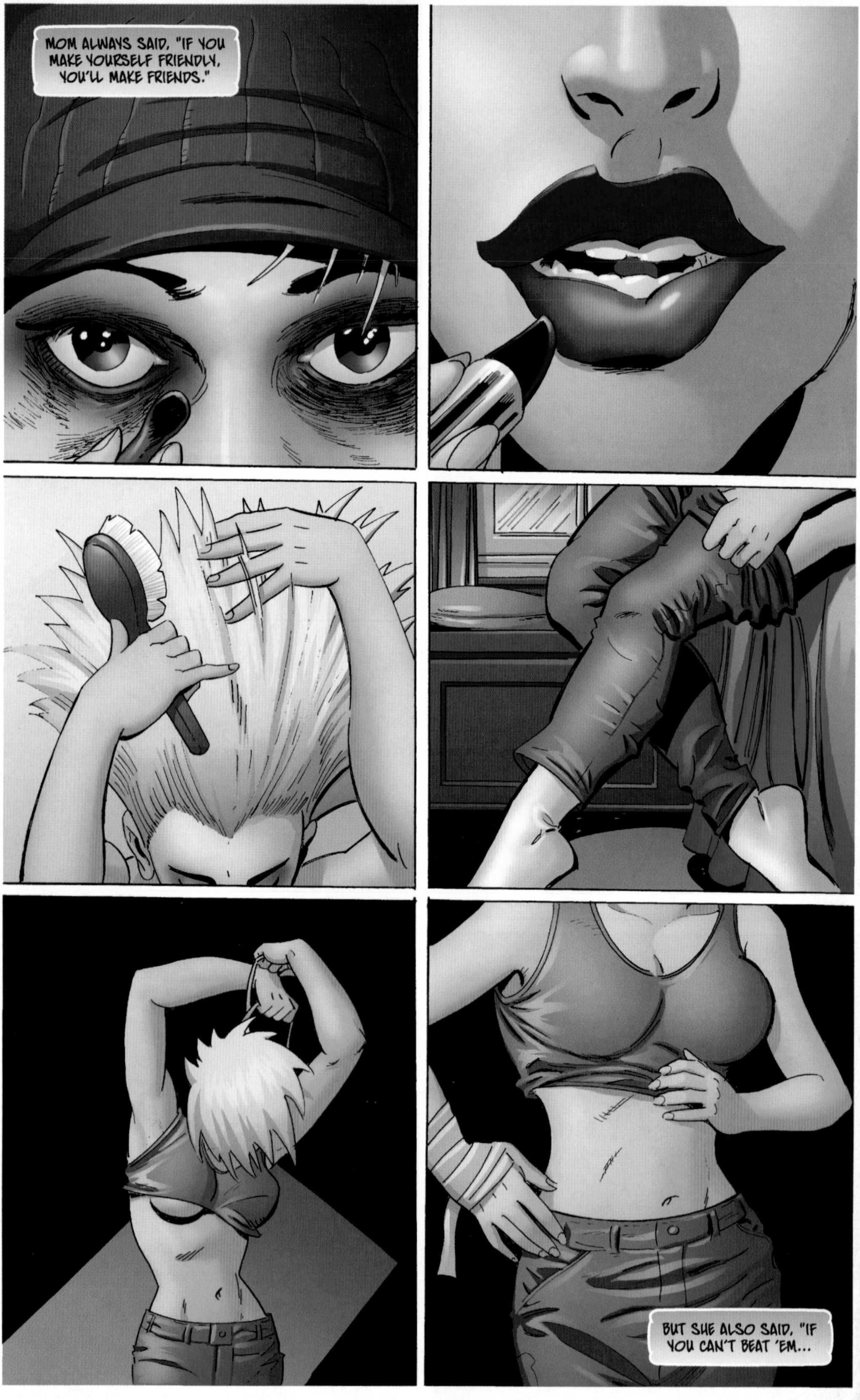
MOM ALWAYS SAID, "IF YOU MAKE YOURSELF FRIENDLY, YOU'LL MAKE FRIENDS."
BUT SHE ALSO SAID, "IF YOU CAN'T BEAT 'EM...

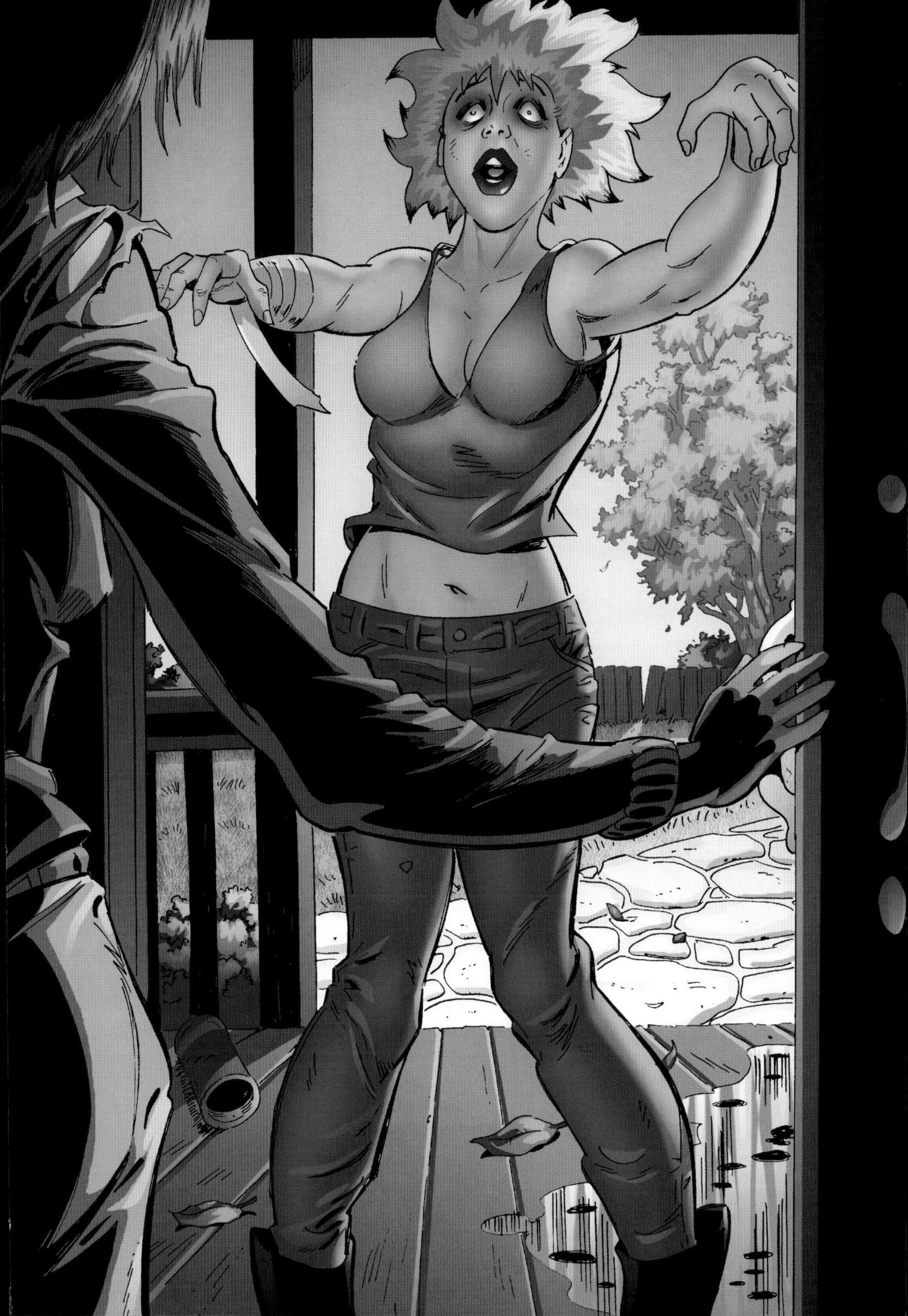

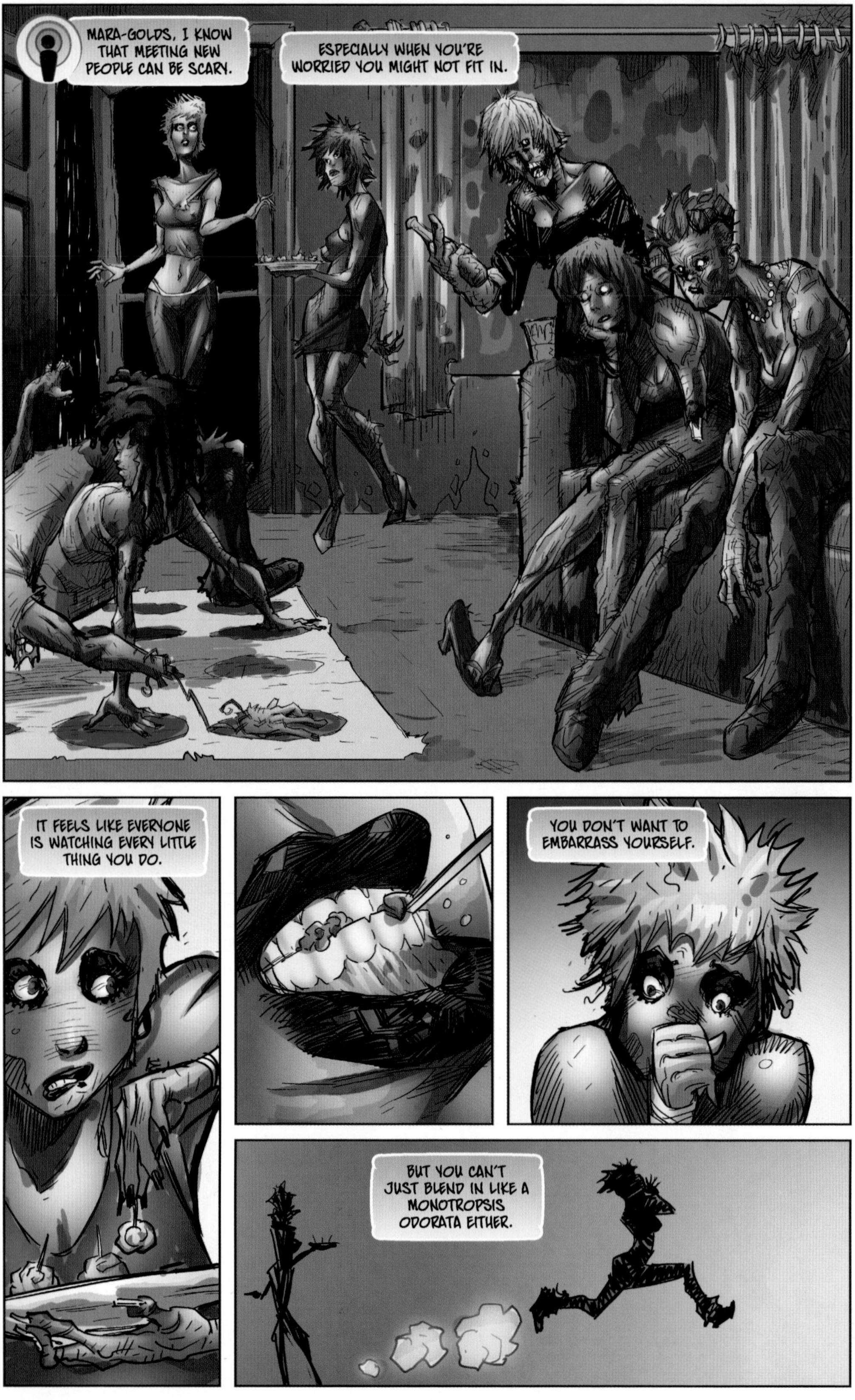
MARA-GOLDS, I KNOW THAT MEETING NEW PEOPLE CAN BE SCARY.
ESPECIALLY WHEN YOU'RE WORRIED YOU MIGHT NOT FIT IN.
IT FEELS LIKE EVERYONE IS WATCHING EVERY LITTLE THING YOU DO.
YOU DON'T WANT TO EMBARRASS YOURSELF.
BUT YOU CAN'T JUST BLEND IN LIKE A MONOTROPSIS ODORATA EITHER.

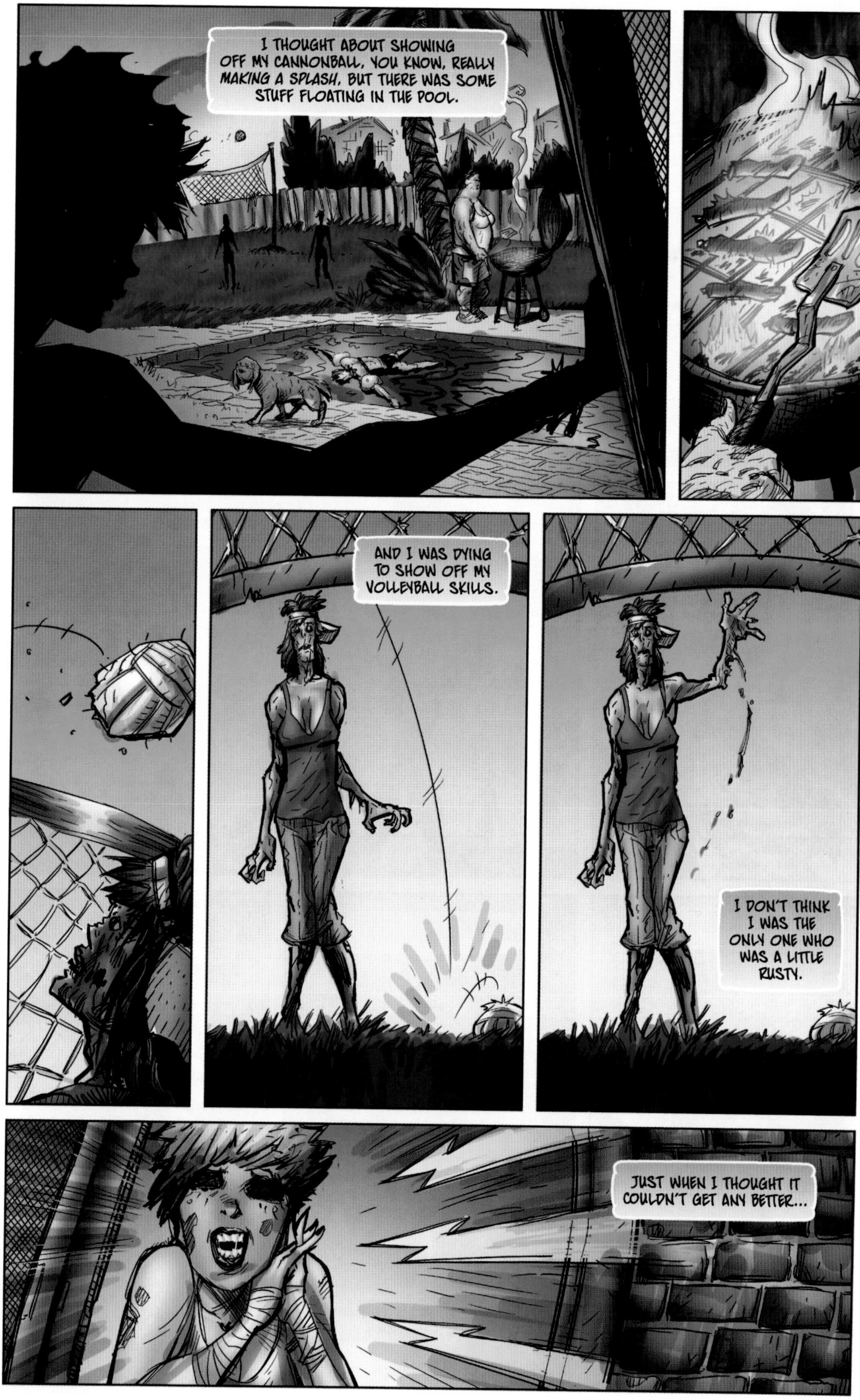
I THOUGHT ABOUT SHOWING OFF MY CANNONBALL, YOU KNOW, REALLY MAKING A SPLASH, BUT THERE WAS SOME STUFF FLOATING IN THE POOL.
AND I WAS DYING TO SHOW OFF MY VOLLEYBALL SKILLS.
I DON'T THINK I WAS THE ONLY ONE WHO WAS A LITTLE RUSTY.
JUST WHEN I THOUGHT IT COULDN'T GET ANY BETTER...

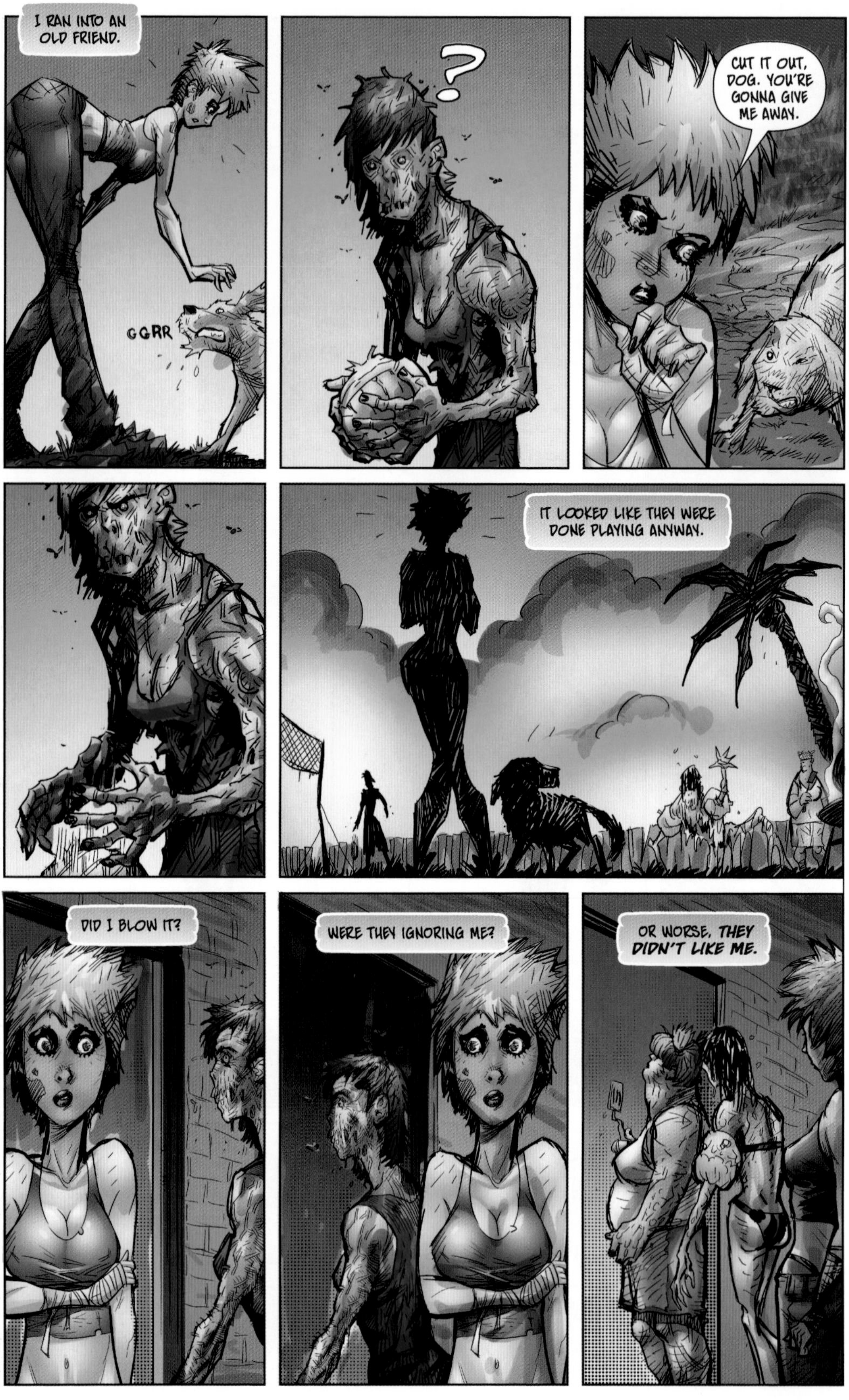
I RAN INTO AN OLD FRIEND.
GGRR
?
CUT IT OUT, DOG. YOU'RE GONNA GIVE ME AWAY.
IT LOOKED LIKE THEY WERE DONE PLAYING ANYWAY.
DID I BLOW IT?
WERE THEY IGNORING ME?
OR WORSE, THEY DIDN'T LIKE ME.

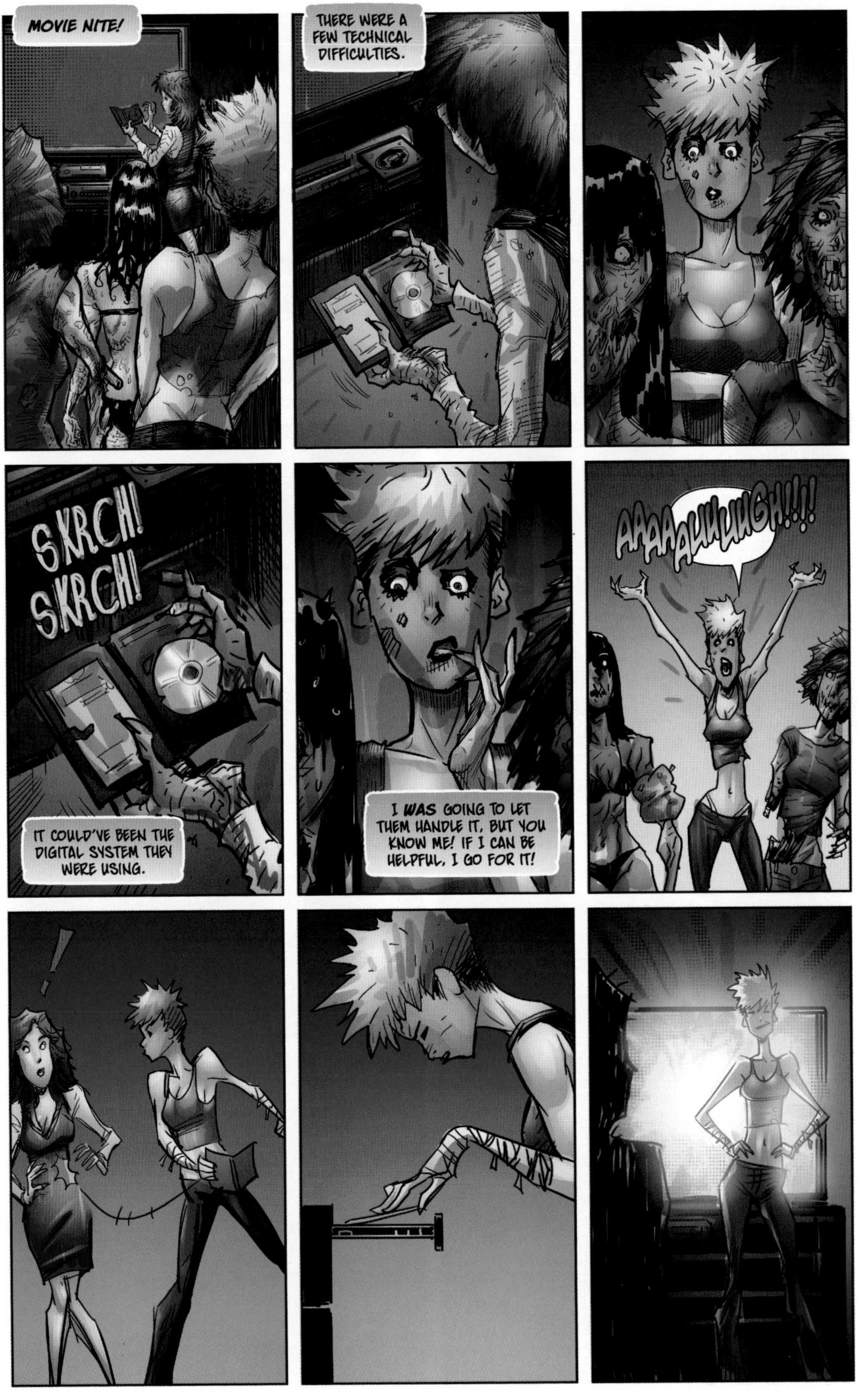
MOVIE NITE!
THERE WERE A FEW TECHNICAL DIFFICULTIES.
SKRCH! SKRCH!
IT COULD'VE BEEN THE DIGITAL SYSTEM THEY WERE USING.
I WAS GOING TO LET THEM HANDLE IT, BUT YOU KNOW ME! IF I CAN BE HELPFUL, I GO FOR IT!
AAAAAHUUUGH!!!!
!

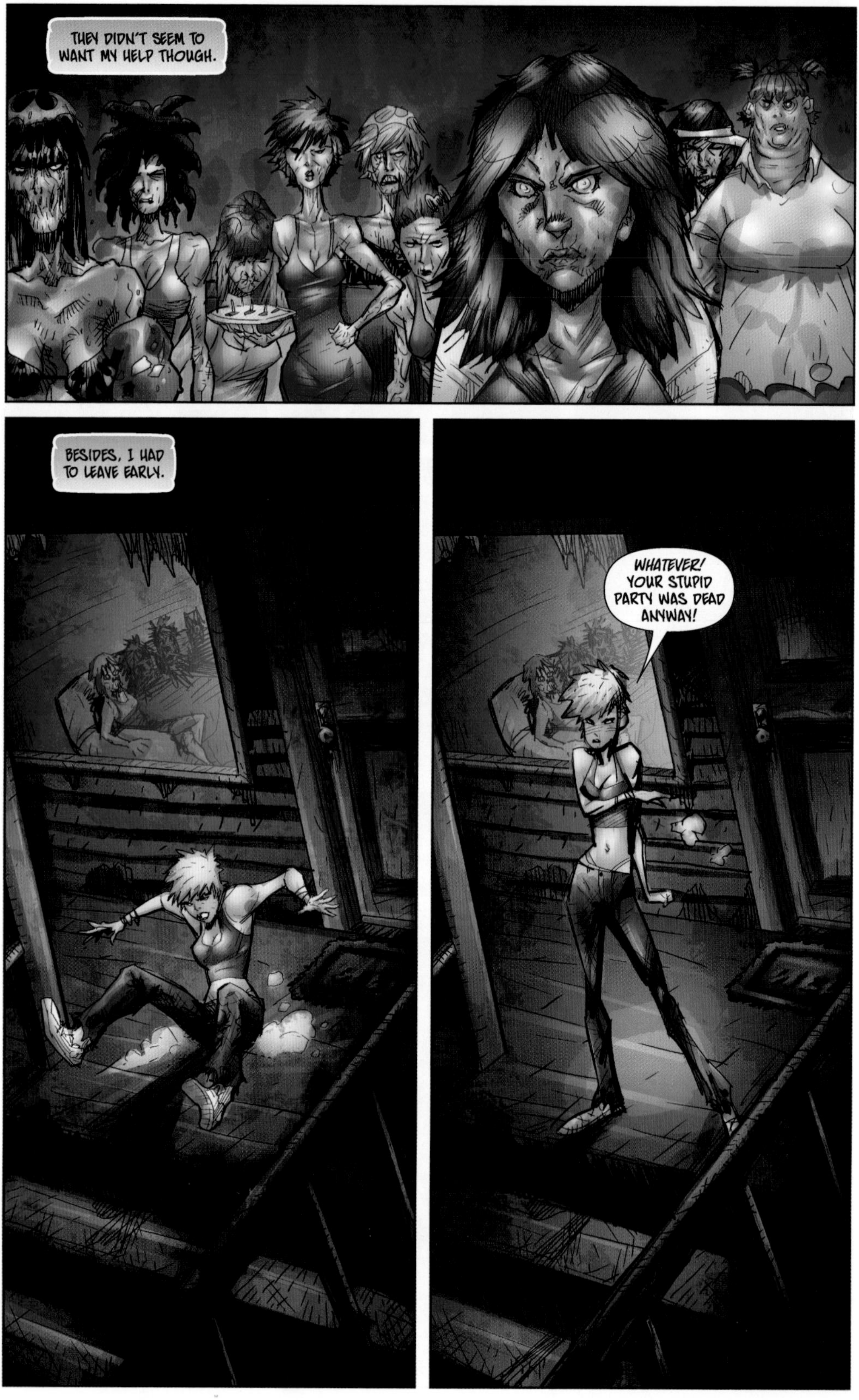
THEY DIDN'T SEEM TO WANT MY HELP THOUGH.
BESIDES, I HAD TO LEAVE EARLY.
WHATEVER! YOUR STUPID PARTY WAS DEAD ANYWAY!

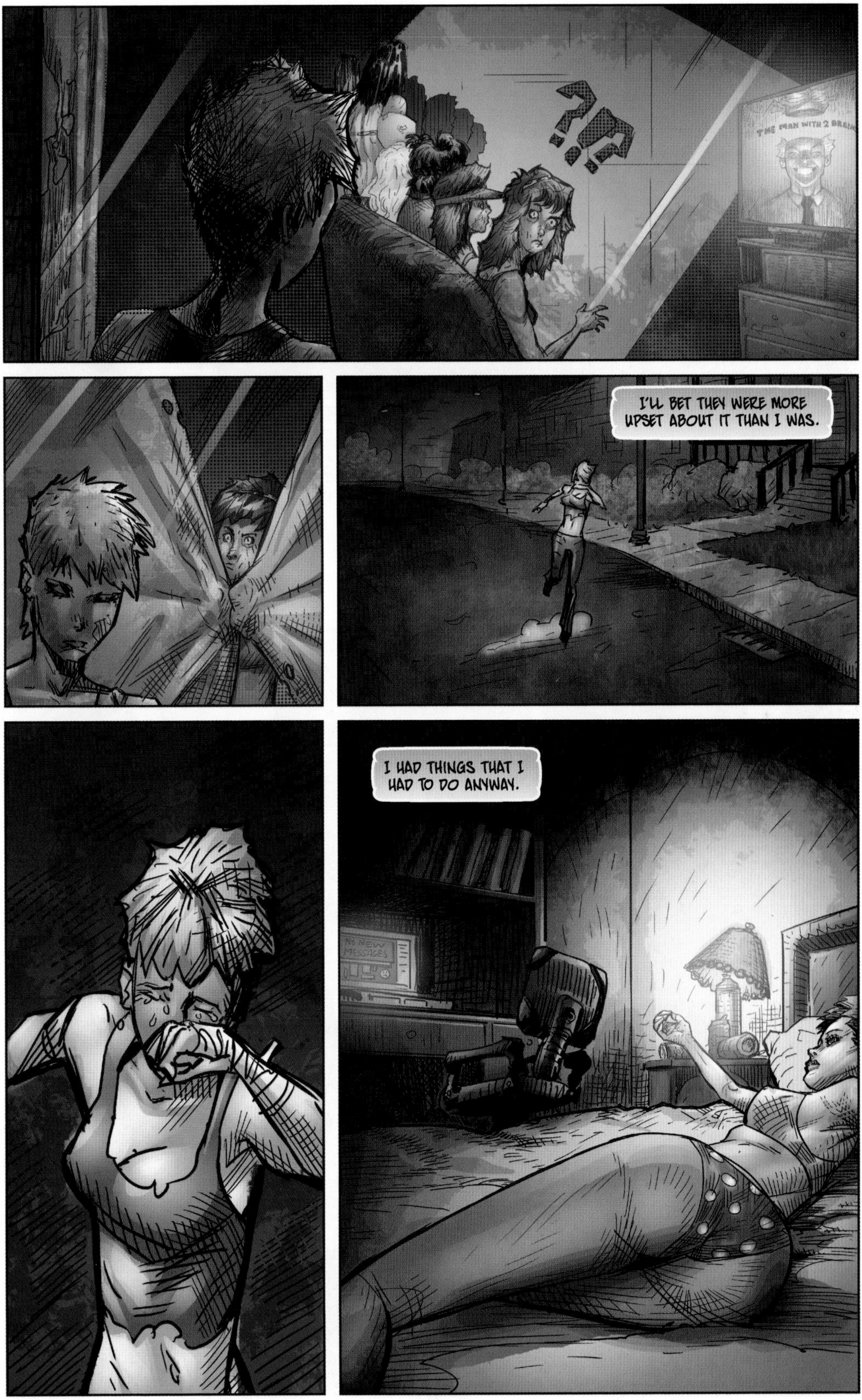
I'LL BET THEY WERE MORE UPSET ABOUT IT THAN I WAS.
I HAD THINGS THAT I HAD TO DO ANYWAY.

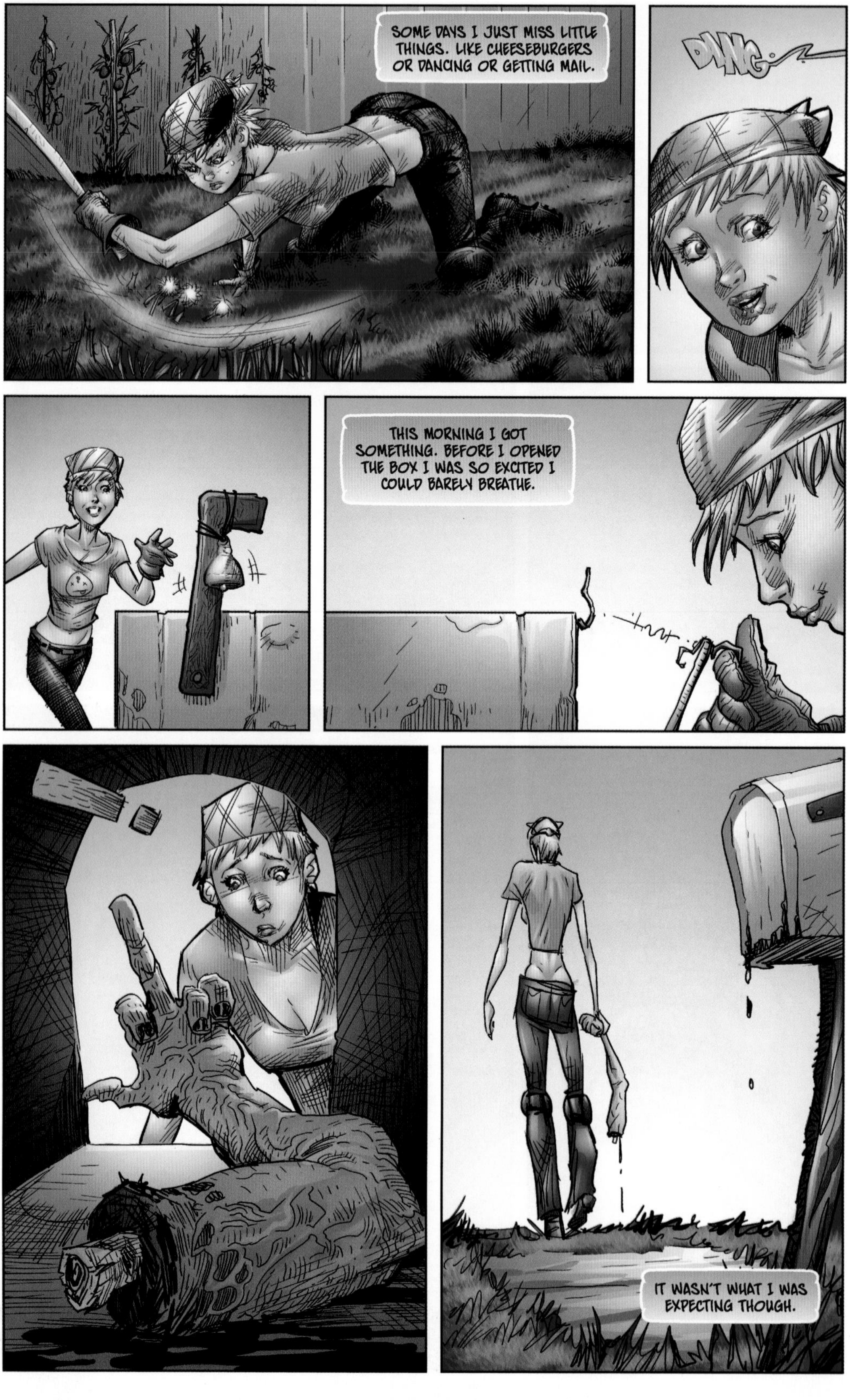
SOME DAYS I JUST MISS LITTLE THINGS. LIKE CHEESEBURGERS OR DANCING OR GETTING MAIL.
DANG
THIS MORNING I GOT SOMETHING. BEFORE I OPENED THE BOX I WAS SO EXCITED I COULD BARELY BREATHE.
IT WASN'T WHAT I WAS EXPECTING THOUGH.

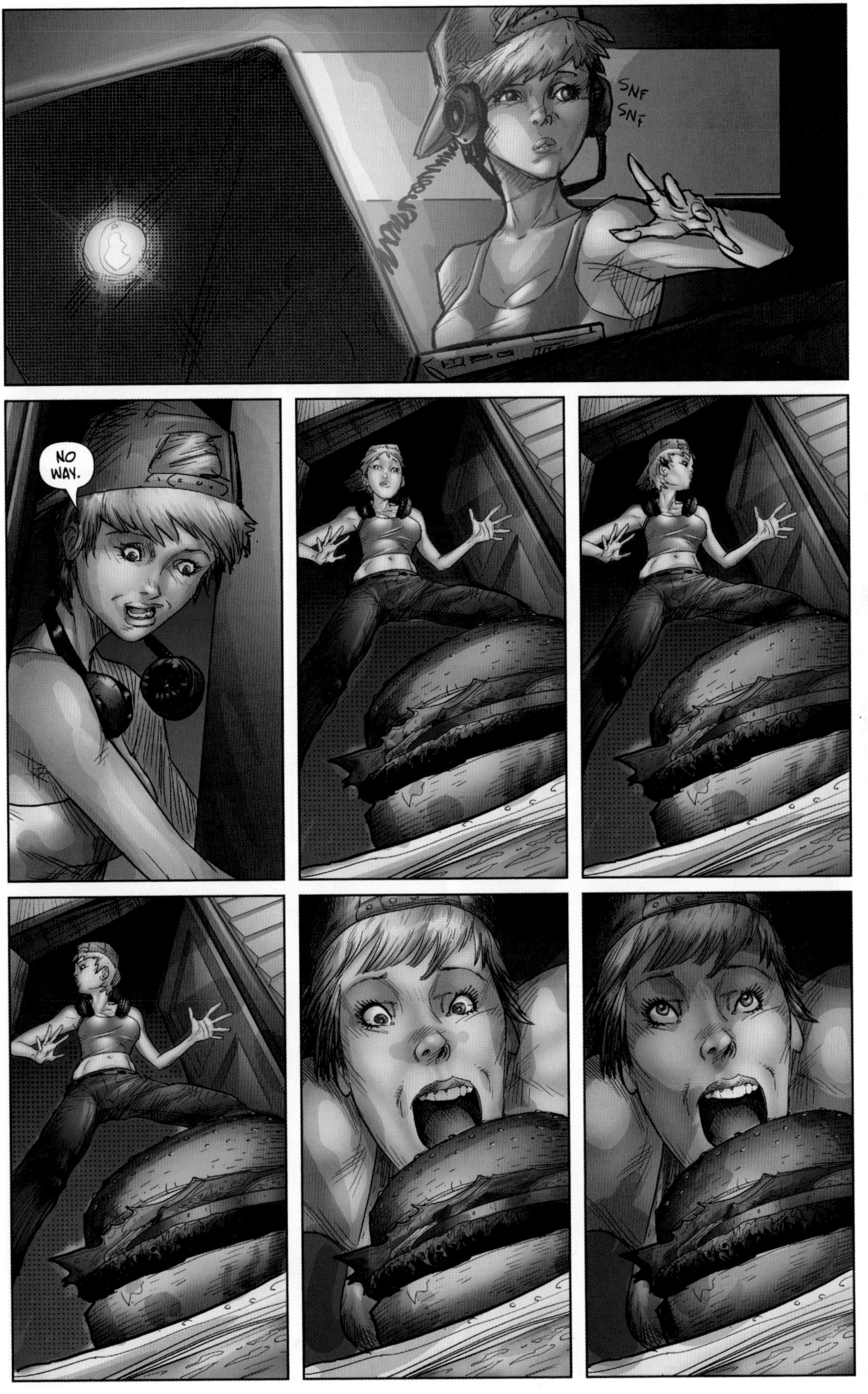
SNF
SNF
NO WAY.

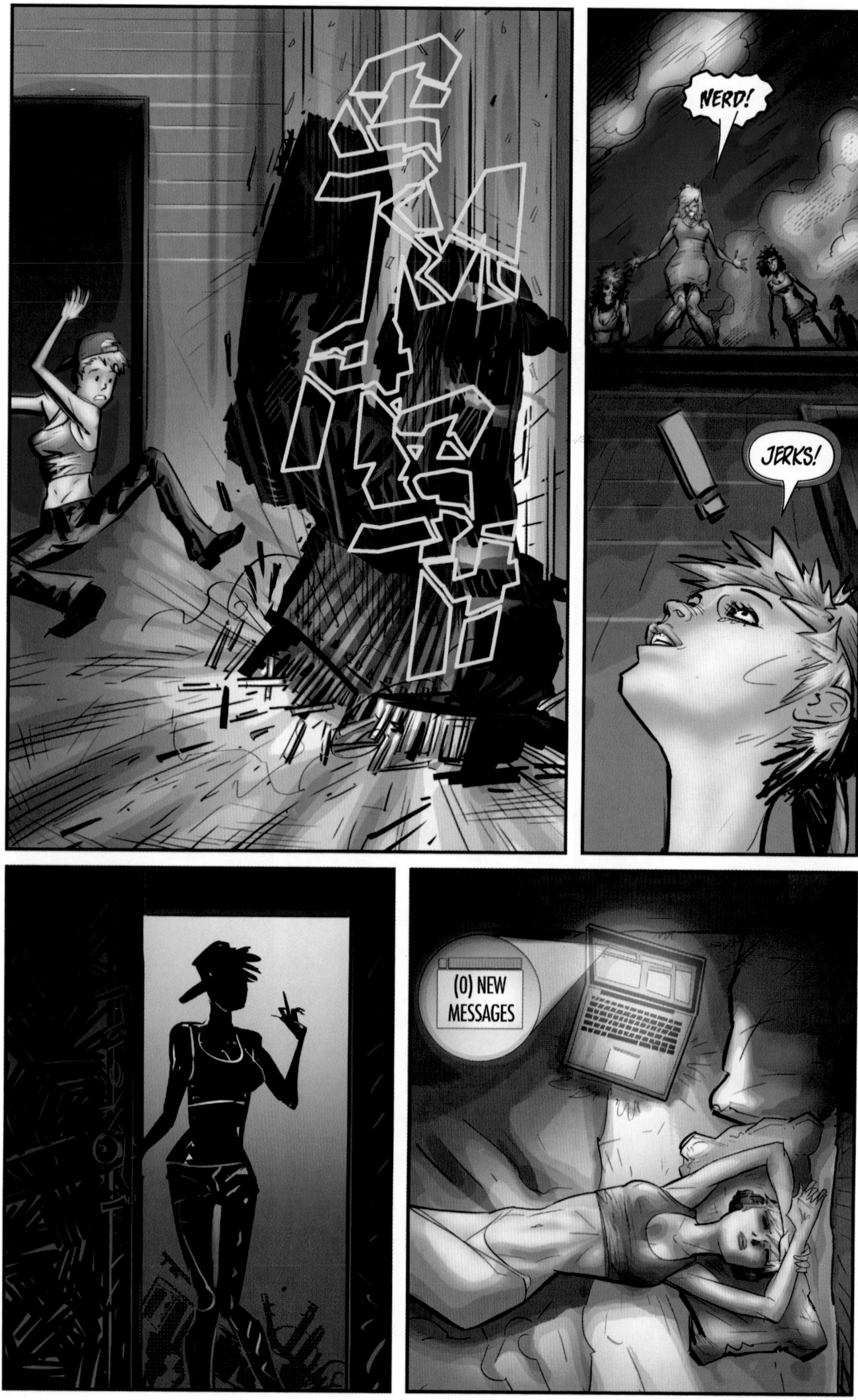
NERD!
JERKS!
(0) NEW MESSAGES

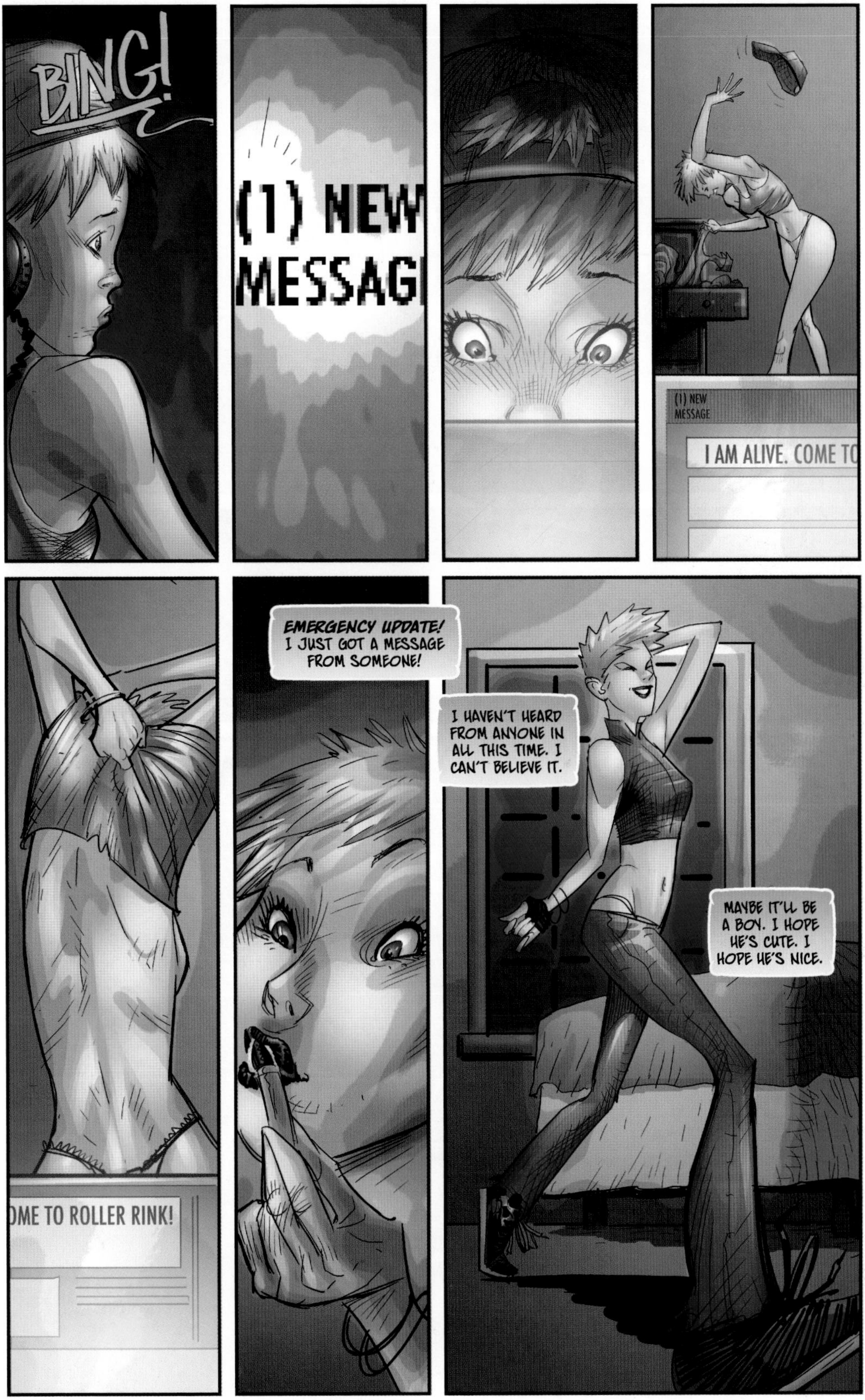
BING!
(1) NEW MESSAGE
(1) NEW MESSAGE
I AM ALIVE. COME TO
OME TO ROLLER RINK!
EMERGENCY UPDATE! I JUST GOT A MESSAGE FROM SOMEONE!
I HAVEN'T HEARD FROM ANYONE IN ALL THIS TIME. I CAN'T BELIEVE IT.
MAYBE IT'LL BE A BOY. I HOPE HE'S CUTE. I HOPE HE'S NICE.

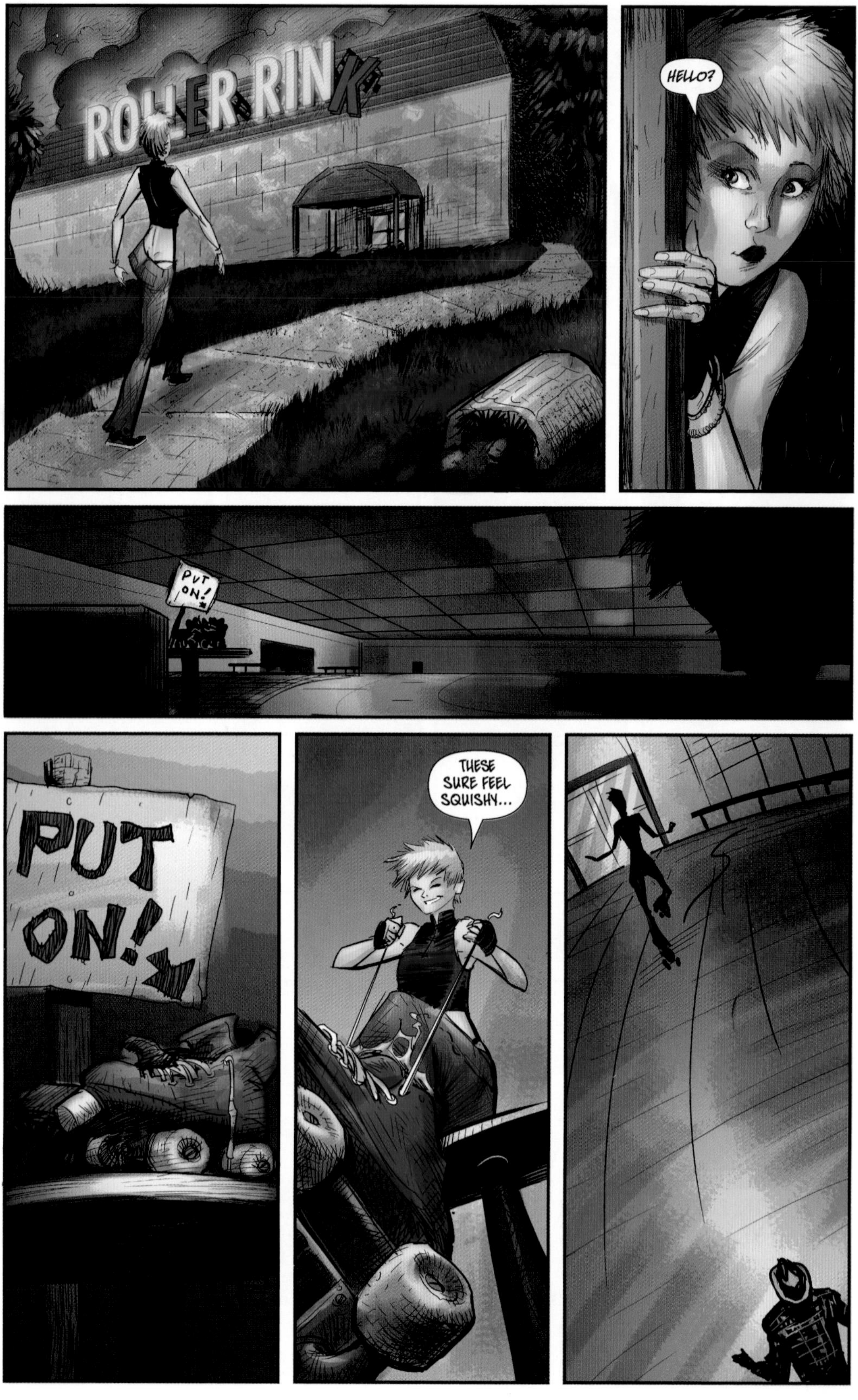
ROLLER RINK
HELLO?
PUT ON!
PUT ON!
THESE SURE FEEL SQUISHY...

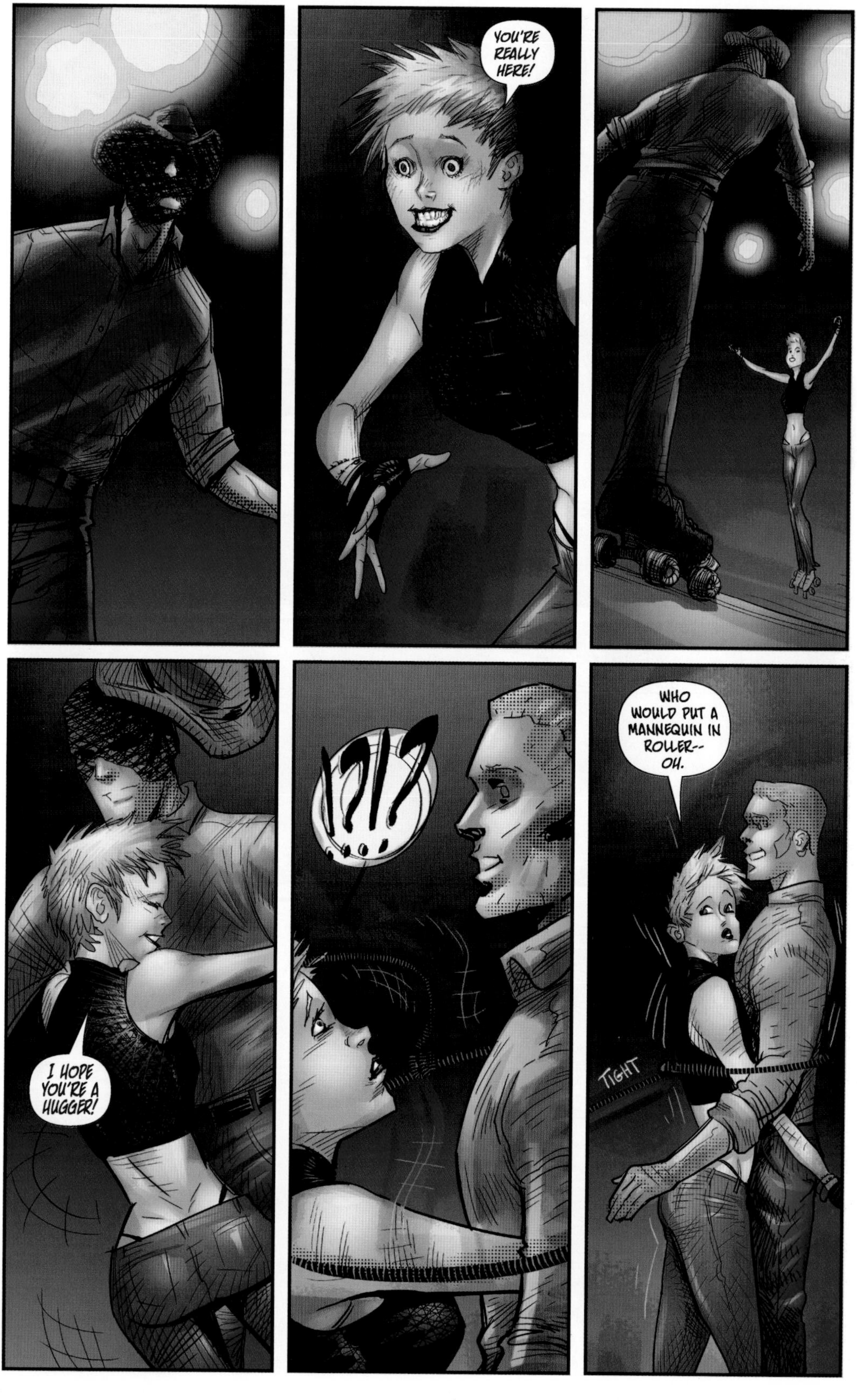
YOU'RE REALLY HERE!
I HOPE YOU'RE A HUGGER!
!?!?...
WHO WOULD PUT A MANNEQUIN IN ROLLER-- OH.
TIGHT

OF COURSE.

BYE.

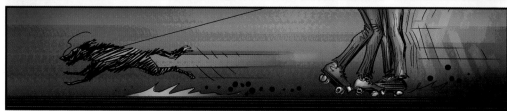

25%

25% GRAD
NEXT 17 M

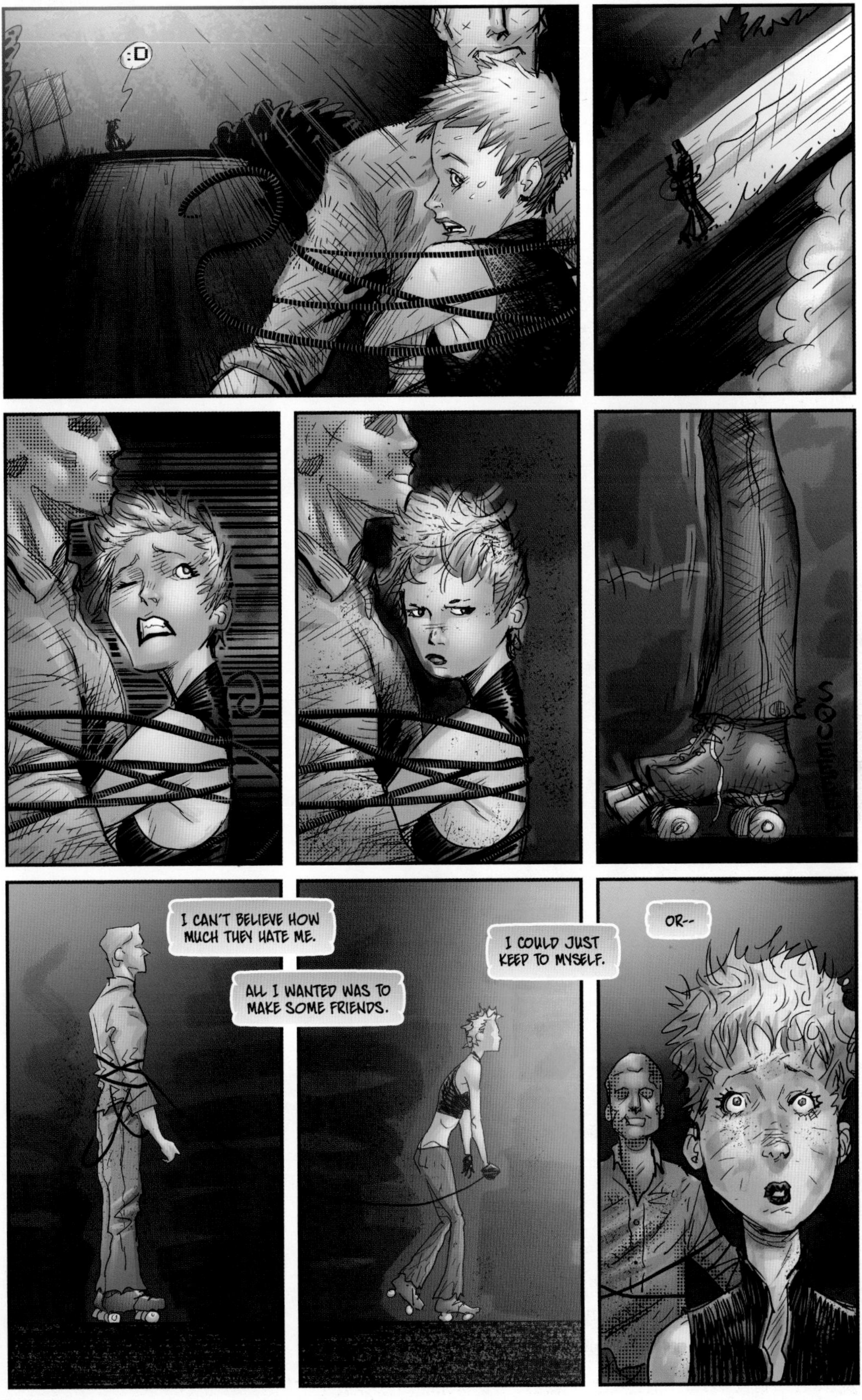
:D
I CAN'T BELIEVE HOW MUCH THEY HATE ME.
ALL I WANTED WAS TO MAKE SOME FRIENDS.
I COULD JUST KEEP TO MYSELF.
OR--

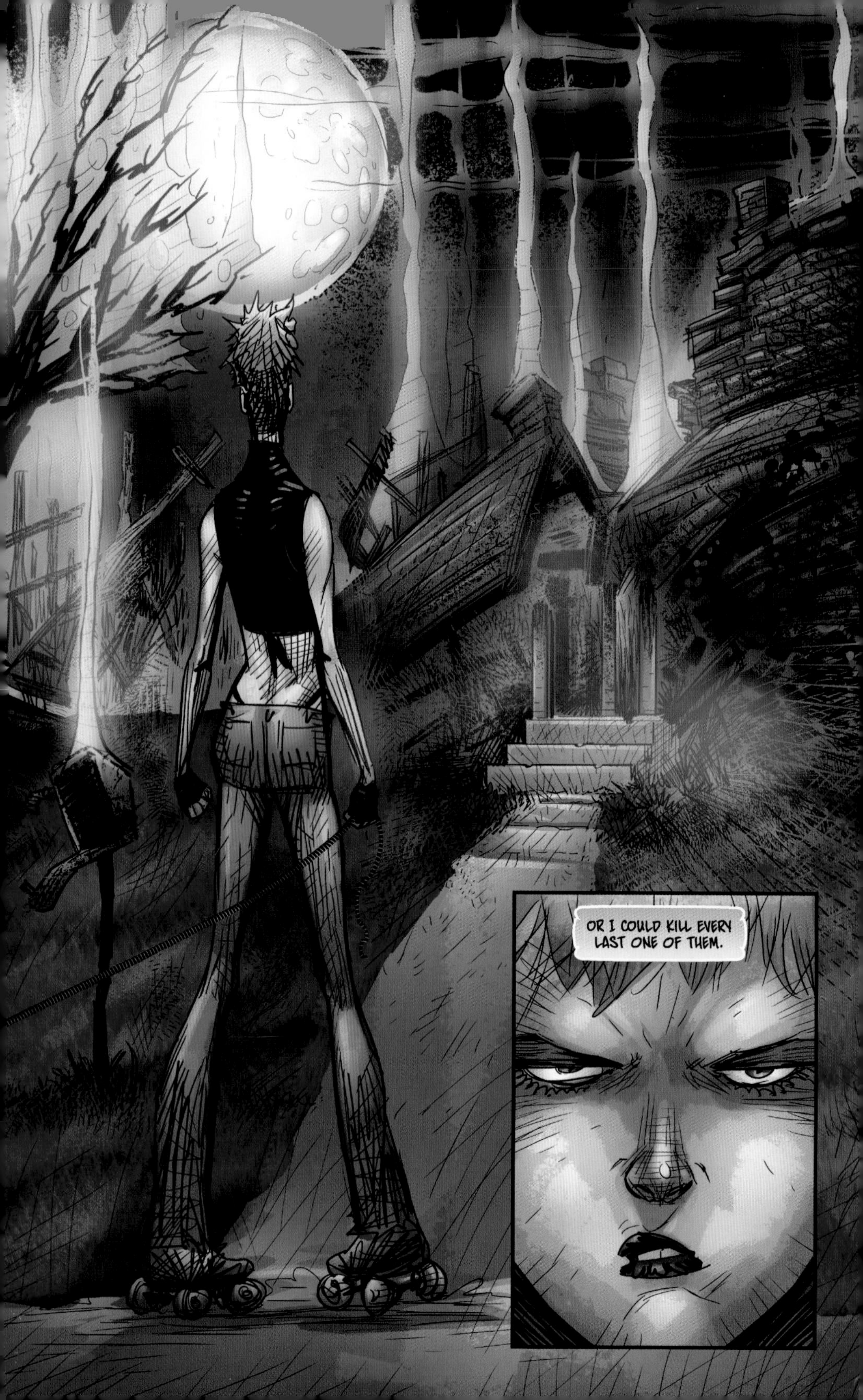
OR I COULD KILL EVERY LAST ONE OF THEM.

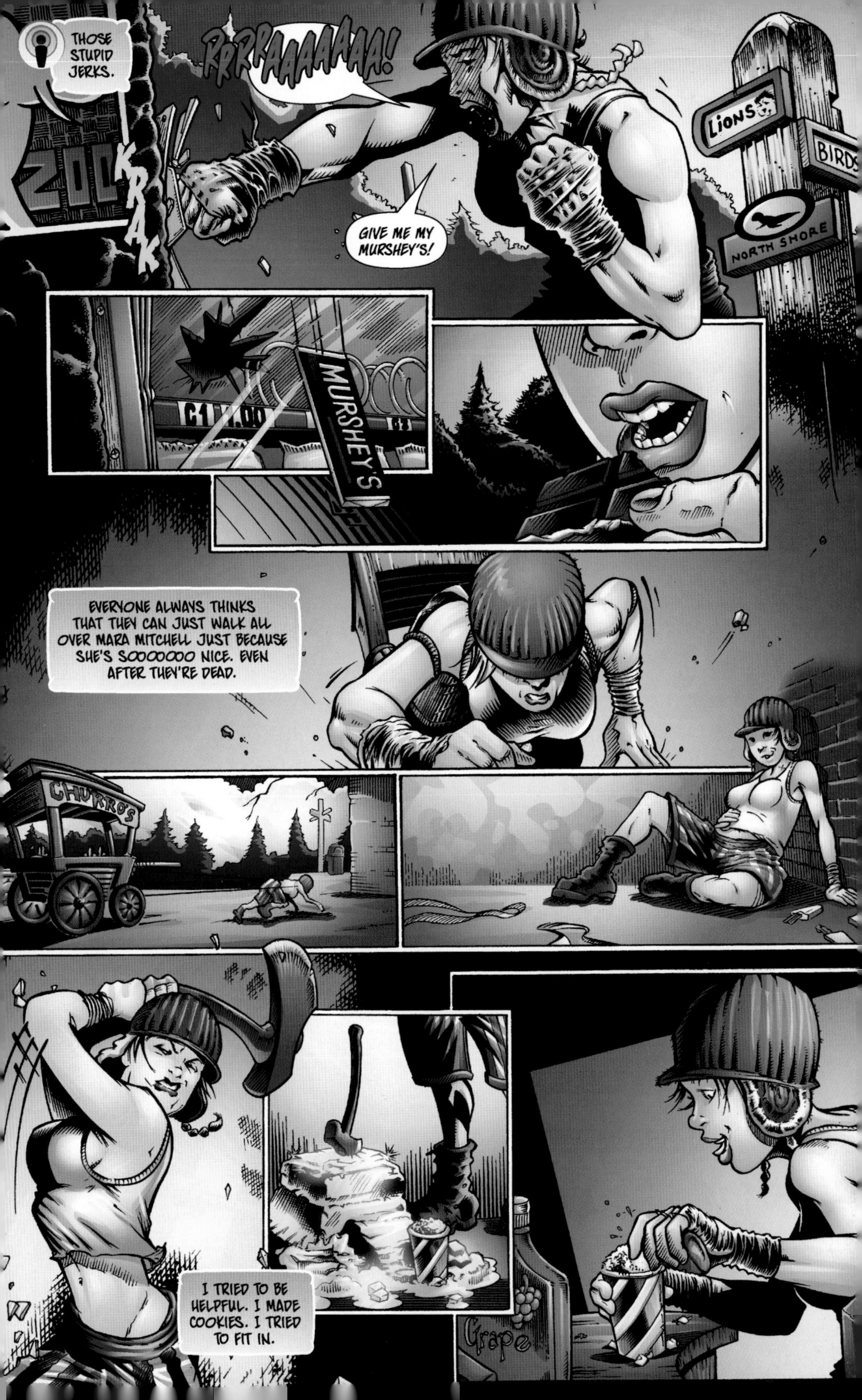
THOSE STUPID JERKS.
RRRRAAAAAAAA!
ZOO
KRAK
LIONS
BIRDS
NORTH SHORE
GIVE ME MY MURSHEY'S!
MURSHEY'S
EVERYONE ALWAYS THINKS THAT THEY CAN JUST WALK ALL OVER MARA MITCHELL JUST BECAUSE SHE'S SOOOOOOO NICE. EVEN AFTER THEY'RE DEAD.
CHURRO'S
I TRIED TO BE HELPFUL. I MADE COOKIES. I TRIED TO FIT IN.
Grape

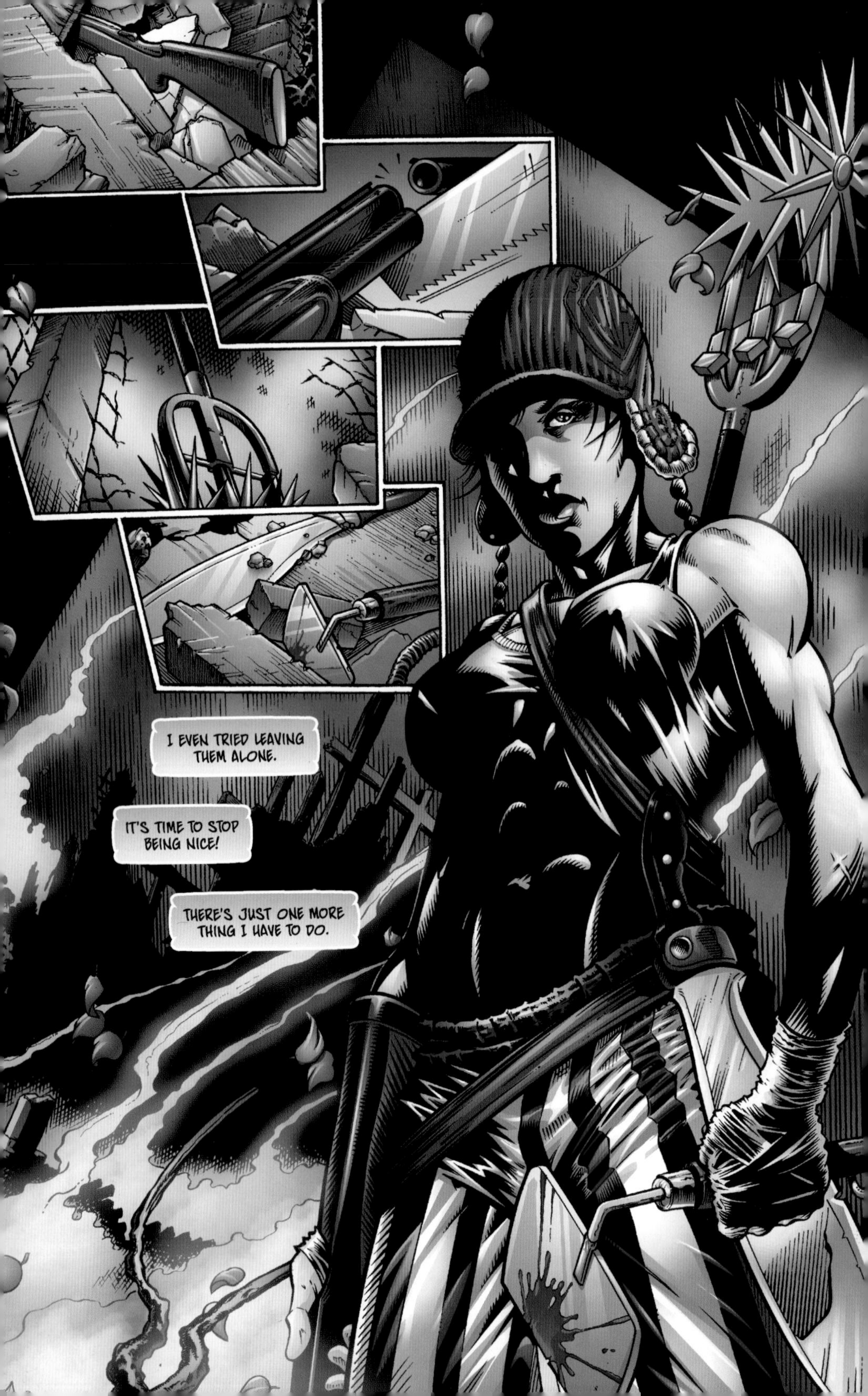
I EVEN TRIED LEAVING THEM ALONE.
IT'S TIME TO STOP BEING NICE!
THERE'S JUST ONE MORE THING I HAVE TO DO.

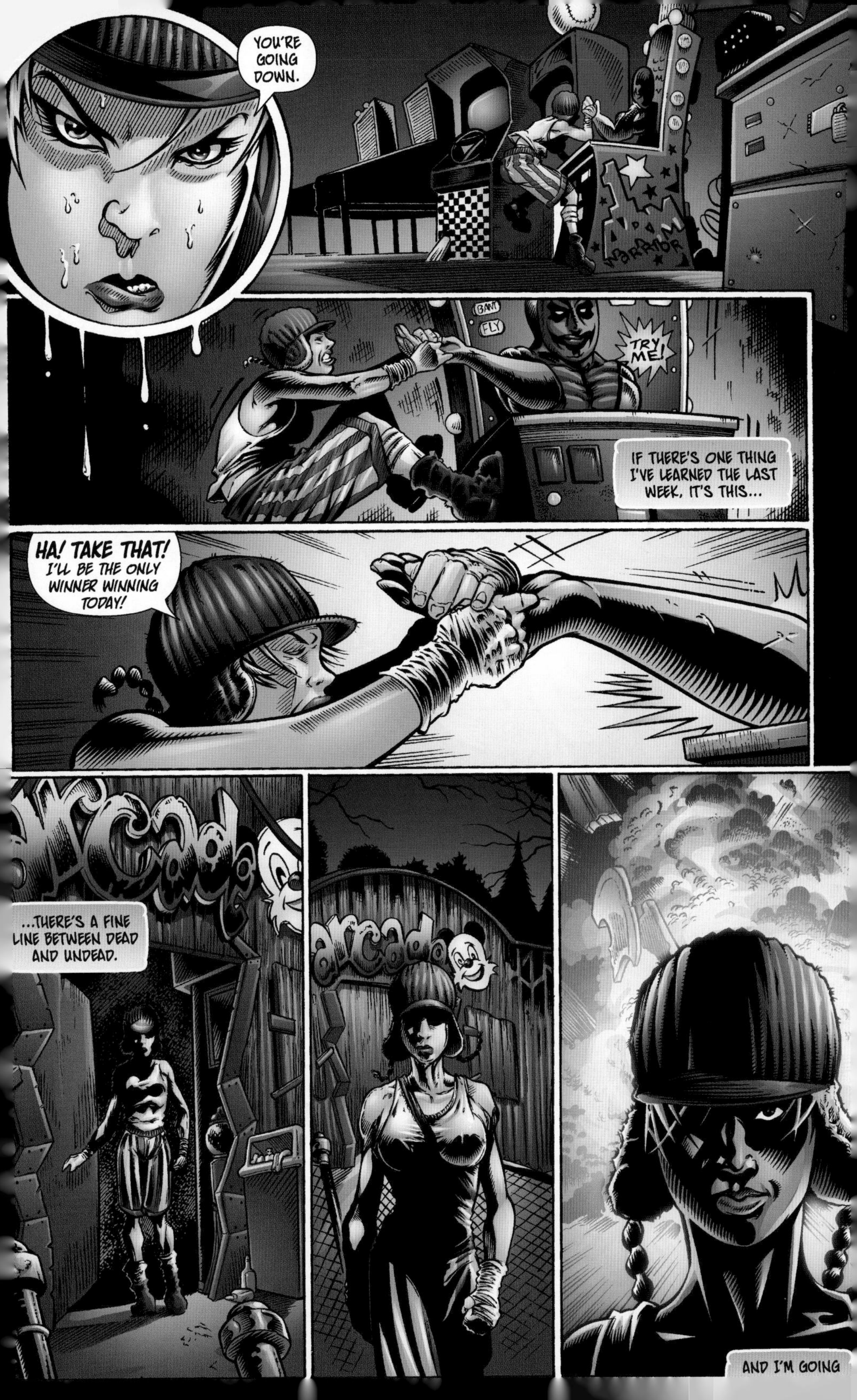
YOU'RE GOING DOWN.
BANT
FLY
WARRIOR
TRY ME!
IF THERE'S ONE THING I'VE LEARNED THE LAST WEEK, IT'S THIS...
HA! TAKE THAT! I'LL BE THE ONLY WINNER WINNING TODAY!
...THERE'S A FINE LINE BETWEEN DEAD AND UNDEAD.
arcade
AND I'M GOING

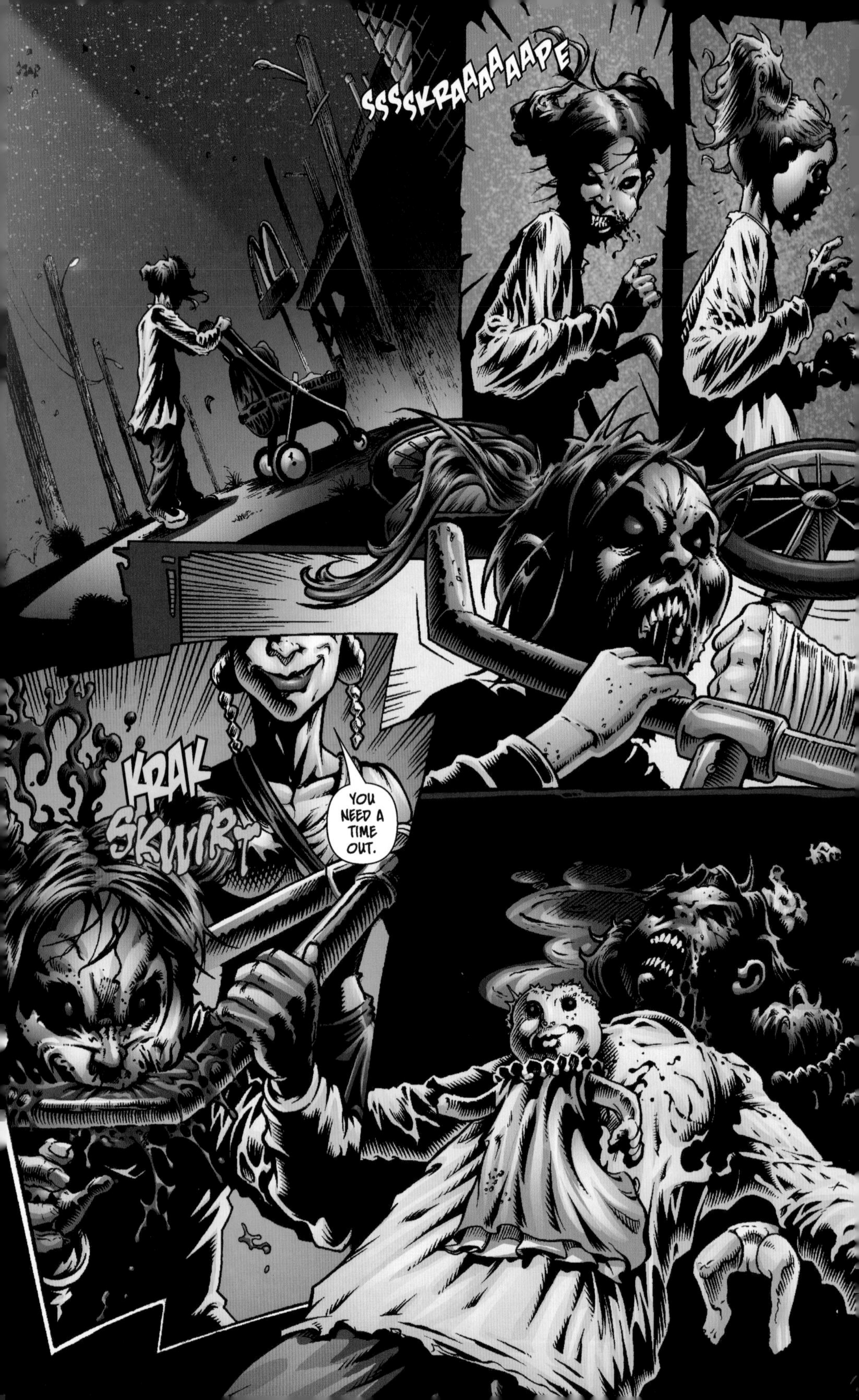
SSSSKRAAAAAAPE
KRAK
SKWIRT
YOU NEED A TIME OUT.

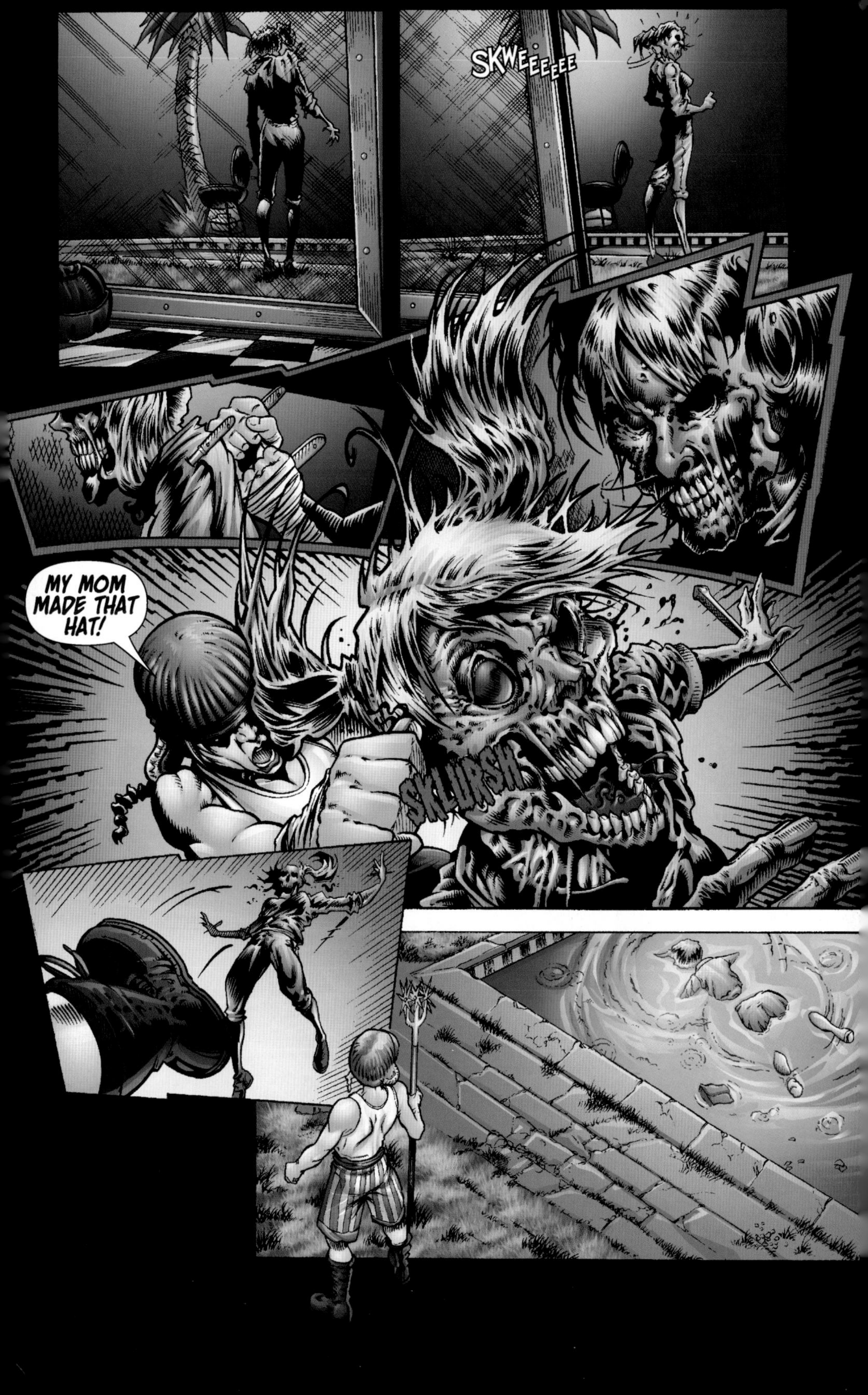
SKWEEEEEE
MY MOM MADE THAT HAT!
SKLURSH

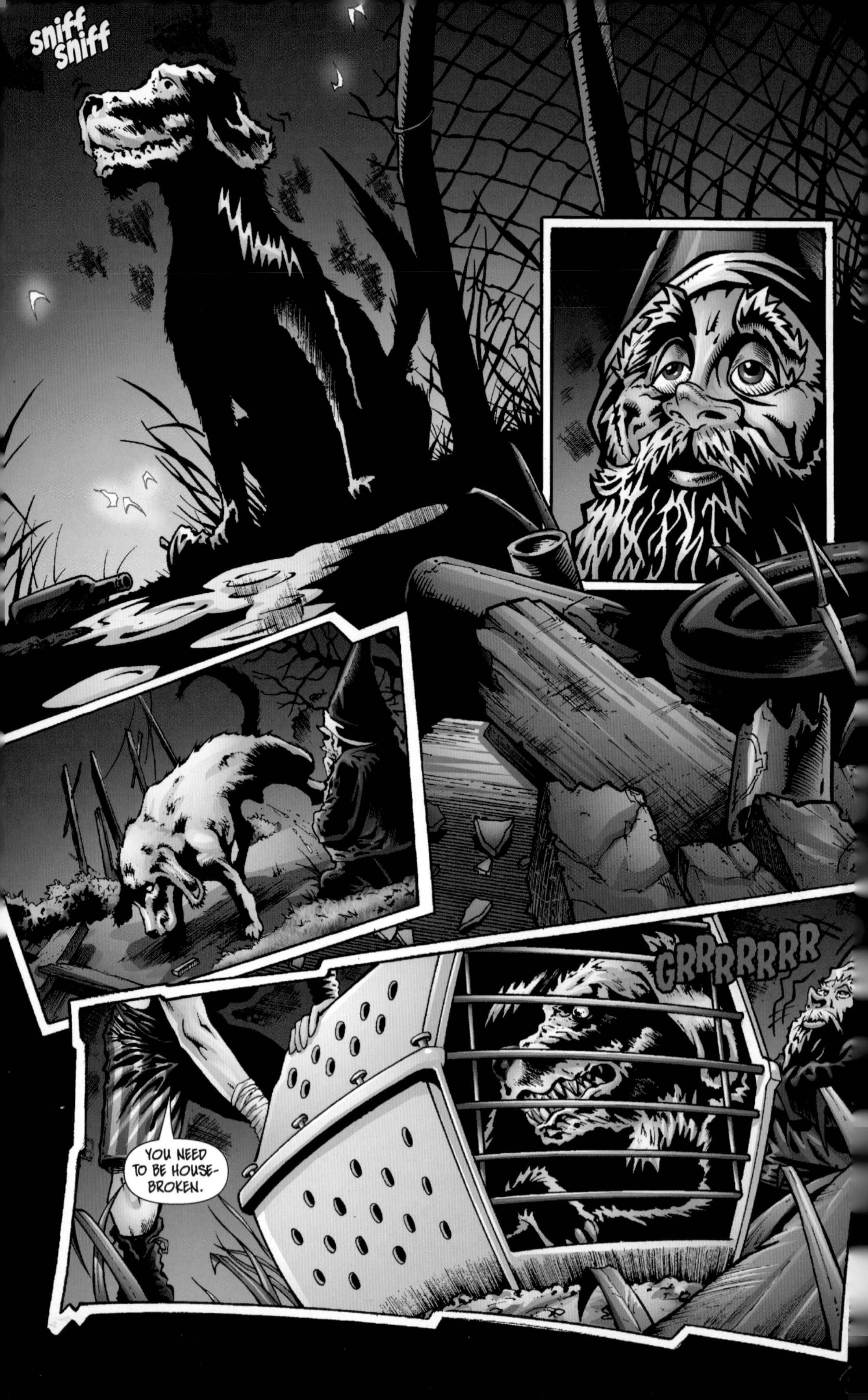
sniff sniff
GRRRRRRR
YOU NEED TO BE HOUSE-BROKEN.

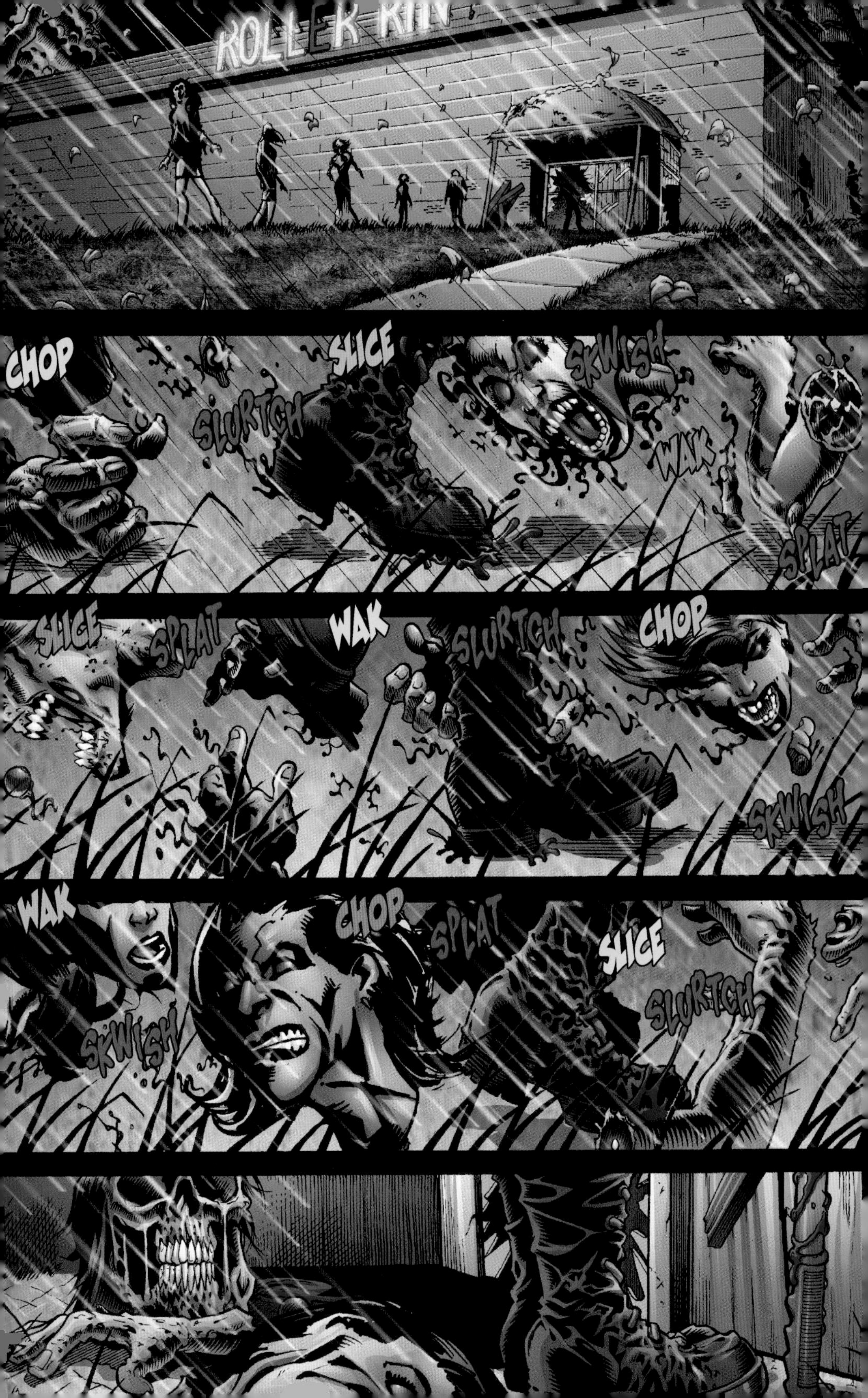
ROLLER RIN
CHOP
SLICE
SLURTCH
SKWISH
WAK
SPLAT
SLICE
SPLAT
WAK
SLURTCH
CHOP
SKWISH
WAK
CHOP
SPLAT
SLICE
SKWISH
SLURTCH

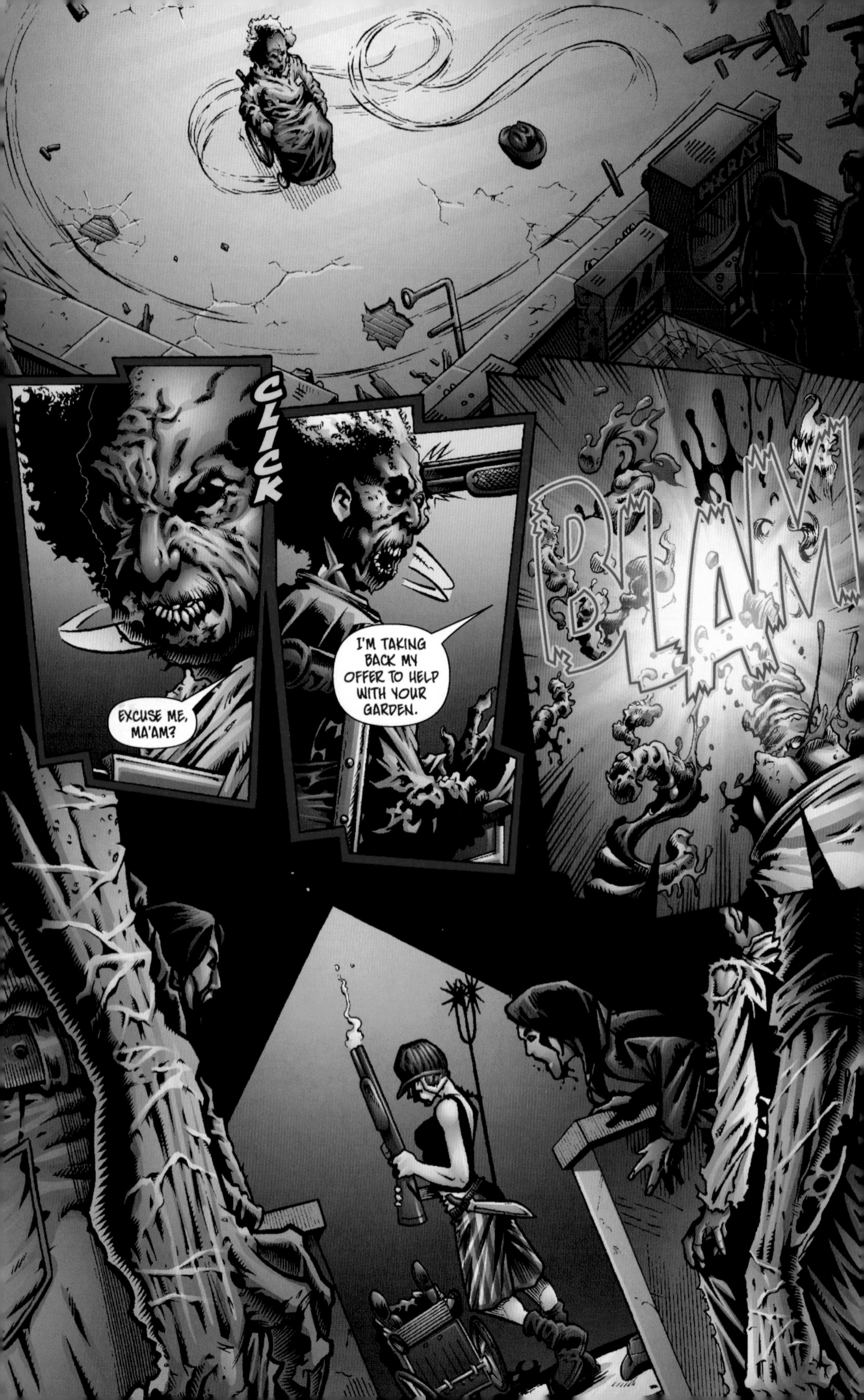

CLICK
EXCUSE ME, MA'AM?
I'M TAKING BACK MY OFFER TO HELP WITH YOUR GARDEN.
BLAM

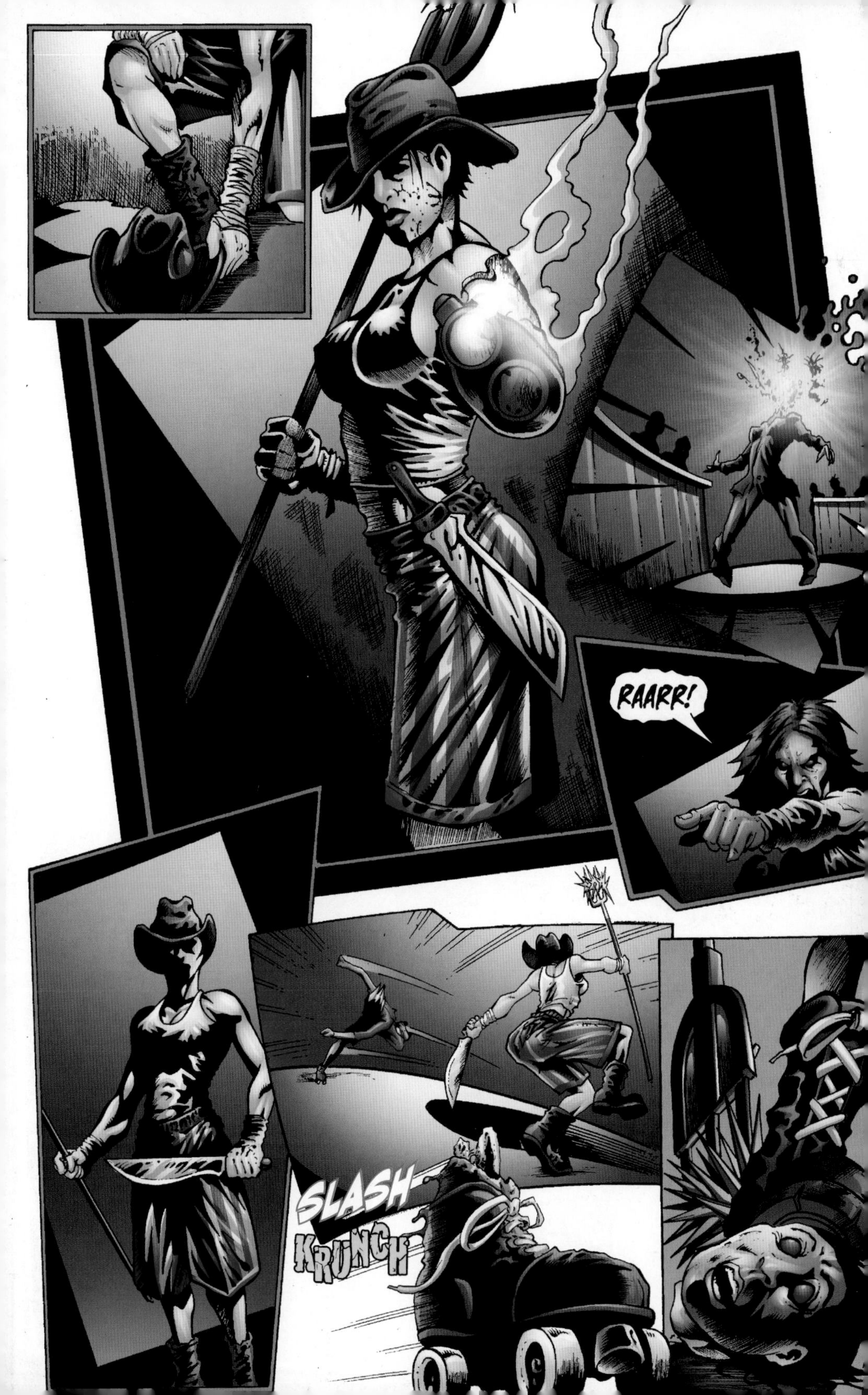

RAARR!
SLASH
KRUNCH

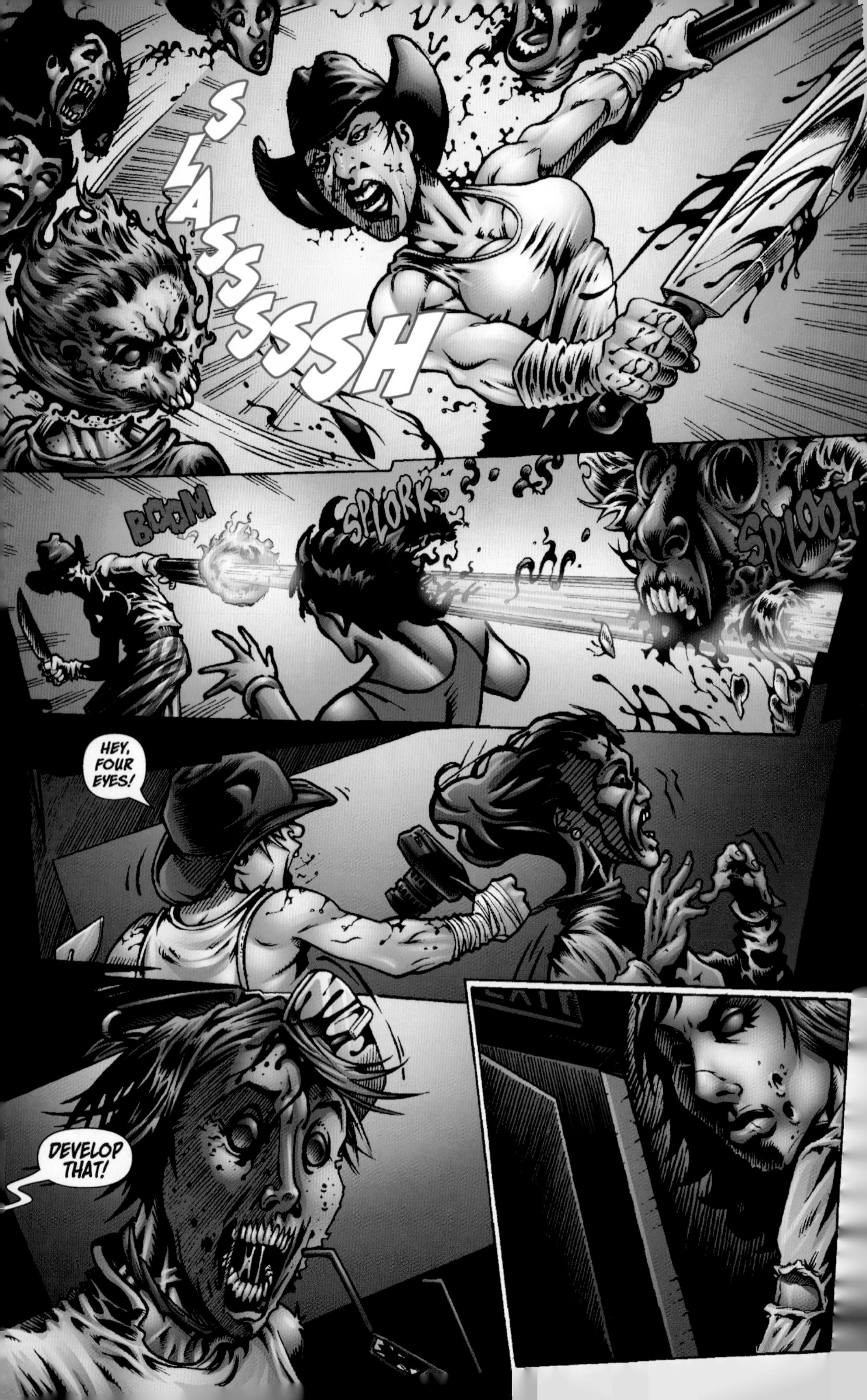
SLASSSSSH
BOOM
SPLORK
SPLOOT
HEY, FOUR EYES!
DEVELOP THAT!

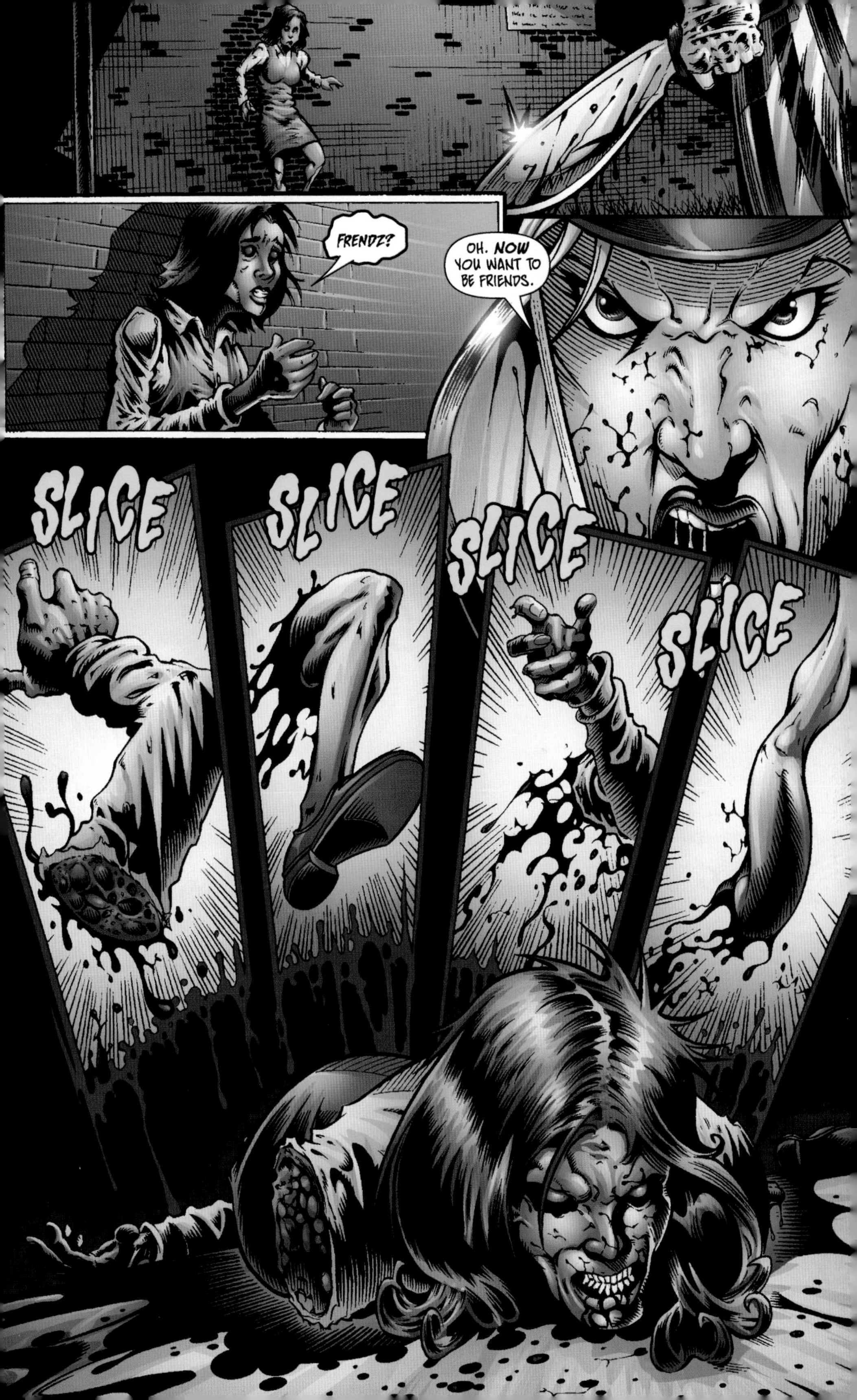
FRENDZ?
OH. NOW YOU WANT TO BE FRIENDS.
SLICE
SLICE
SLICE
SLICE

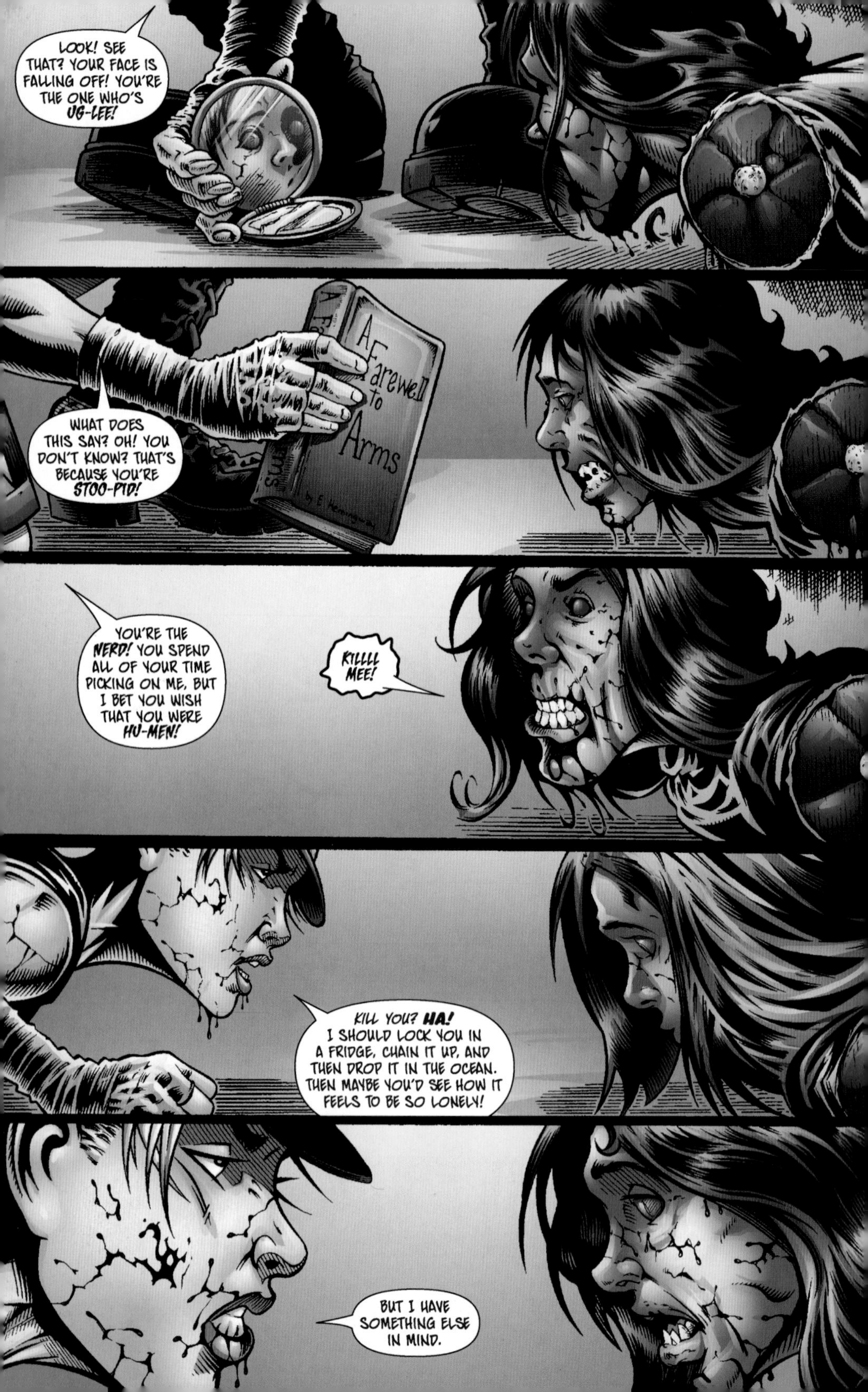
LOOK! SEE THAT? YOUR FACE IS FALLING OFF! YOU'RE THE ONE WHO'S UG-LEE!
A Farewell to Arms
WHAT DOES THIS SAY? OH! YOU DON'T KNOW? THAT'S BECAUSE YOU'RE STOO-PID!
KILLLL MEE!
YOU'RE THE NERD! YOU SPEND ALL OF YOUR TIME PICKING ON ME, BUT I BET YOU WISH THAT YOU WERE HU-MEN!
KILL YOU? HA! I SHOULD LOCK YOU IN A FRIDGE, CHAIN IT UP, AND THEN DROP IT IN THE OCEAN. THEN MAYBE YOU'D SEE HOW IT FEELS TO BE SO LONELY!
BUT I HAVE SOMETHING ELSE IN MIND.

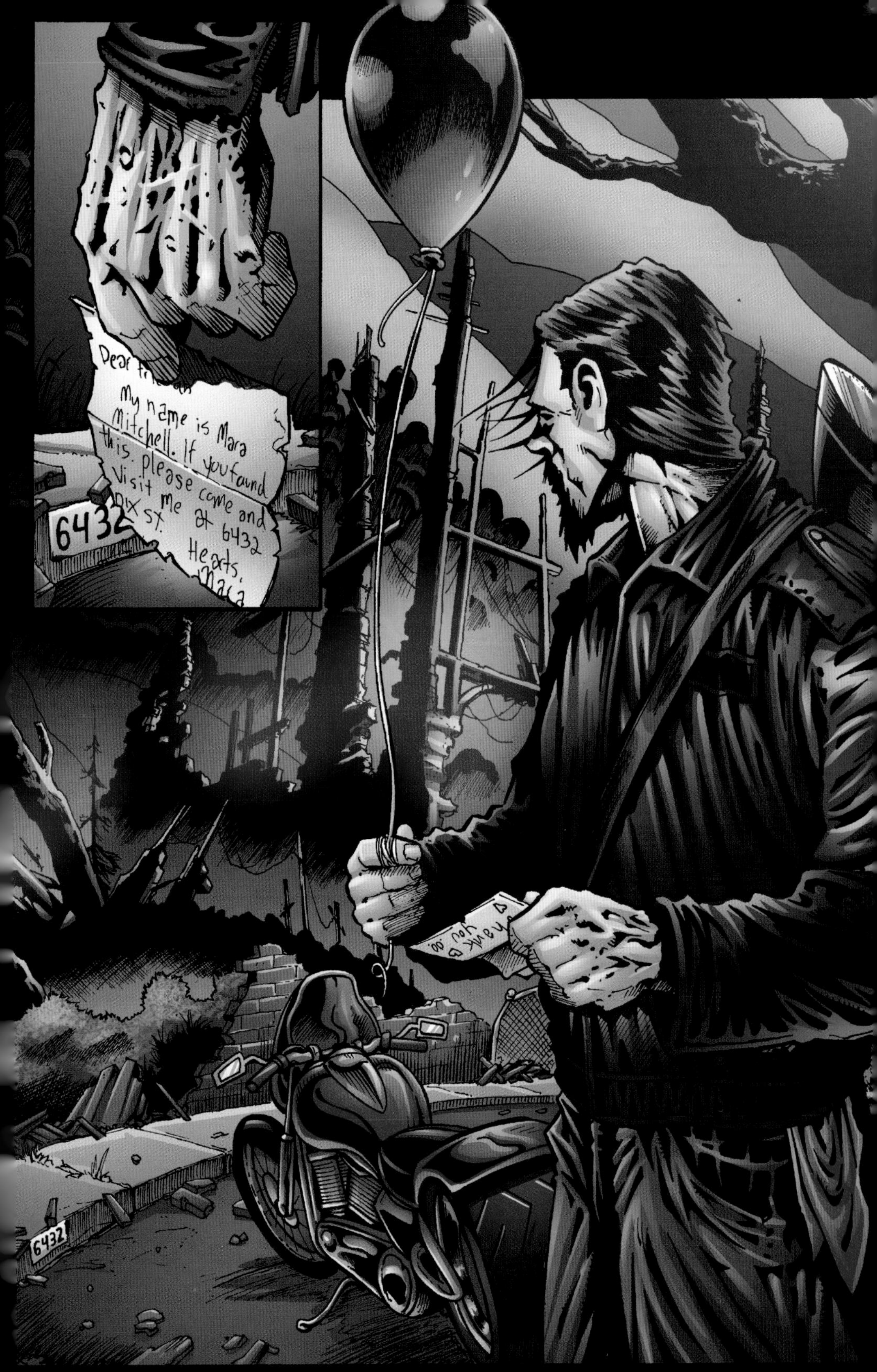
Dear fr
My name is Mara
Mitchell. If you found
this. please come and
Visit me at 6432
Dix St.
Hearts,
Mara
6432
6432

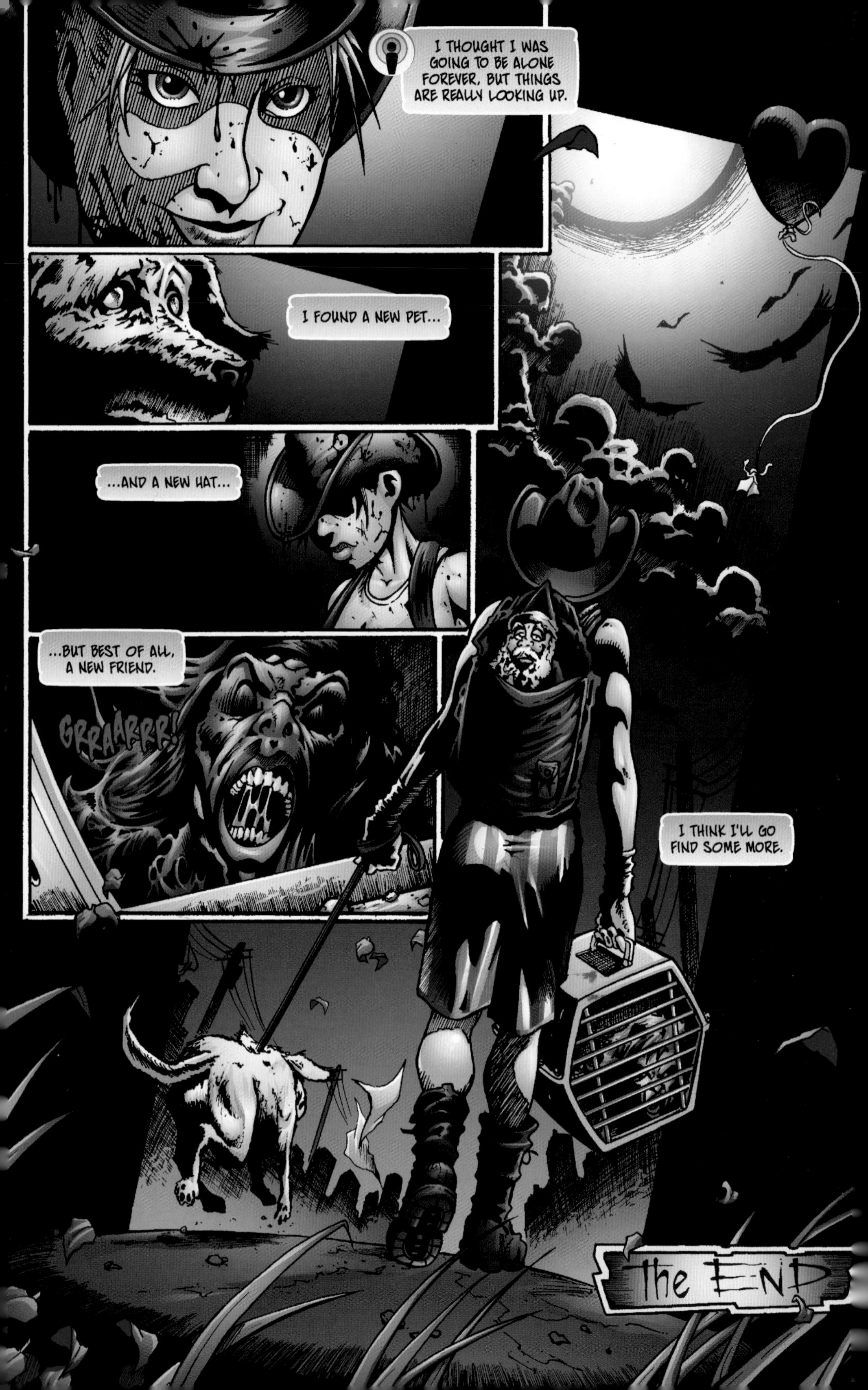
I THOUGHT I WAS GOING TO BE ALONE FOREVER, BUT THINGS ARE REALLY LOOKING UP.
I FOUND A NEW PET...
...AND A NEW HAT...
...BUT BEST OF ALL, A NEW FRIEND.
GRRAARRR!
I THINK I'LL GO FIND SOME MORE.
The END

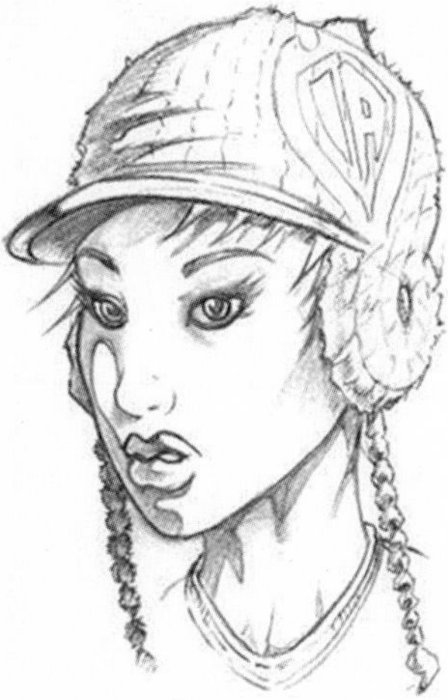

SO... I SURVIVED THE

ZOMBIE APOCALYPSE

AND ALL I GOT WAS THIS PODCAST™ SKETCHBOOK

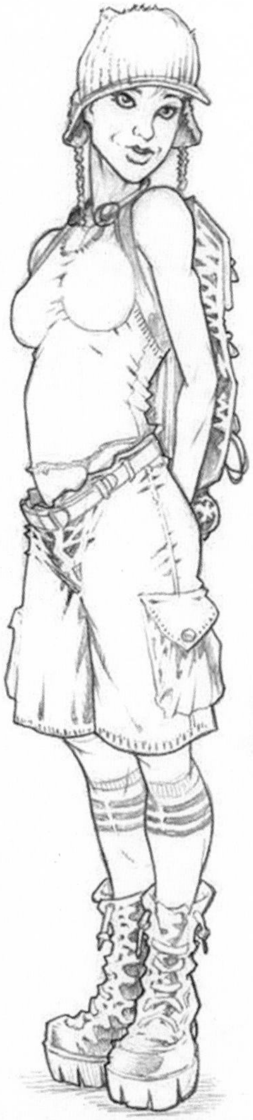

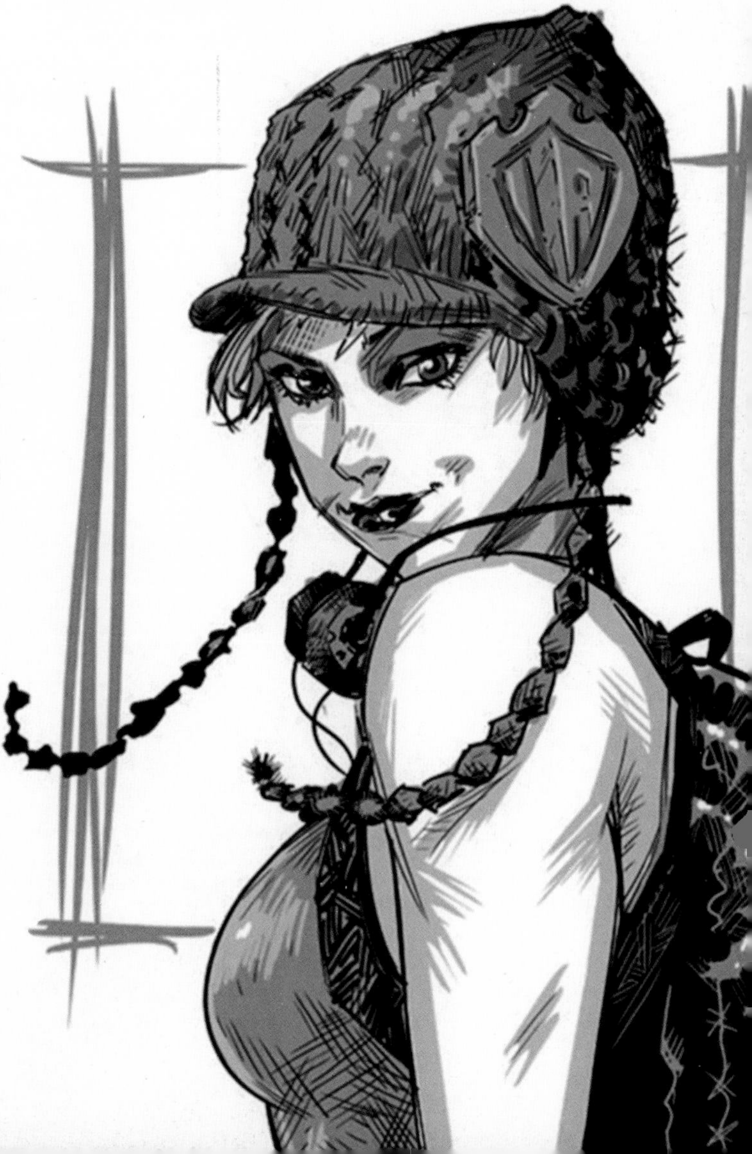

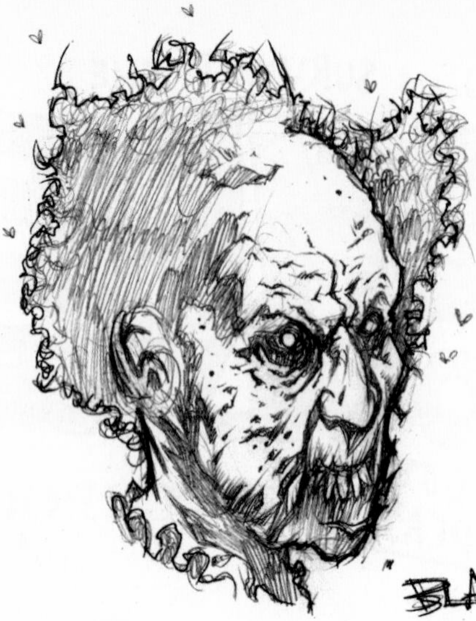

"BLANCHE"

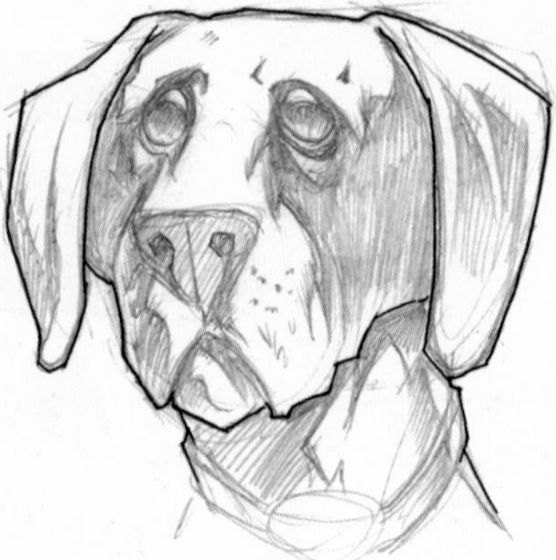

"DOG"

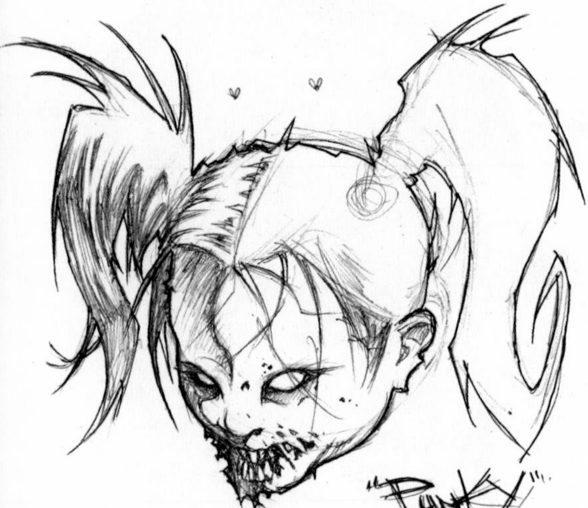

"PUNKY"

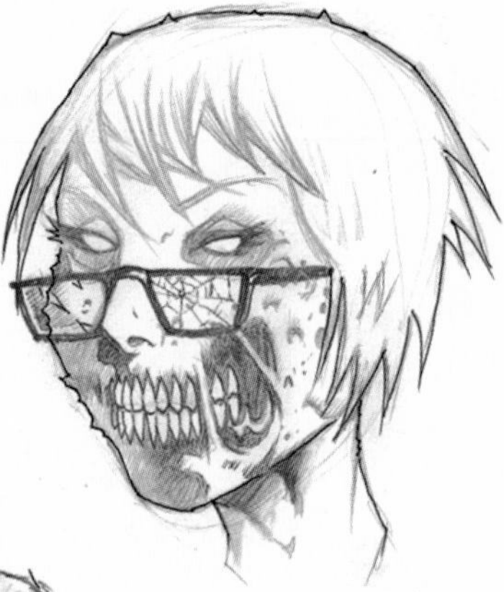

"LIZ"

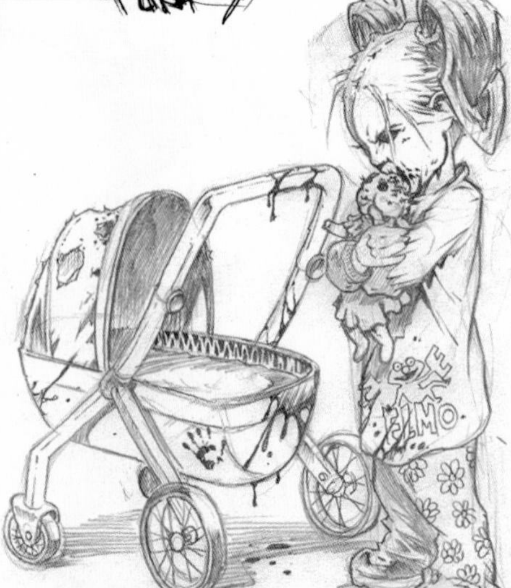
ELMO

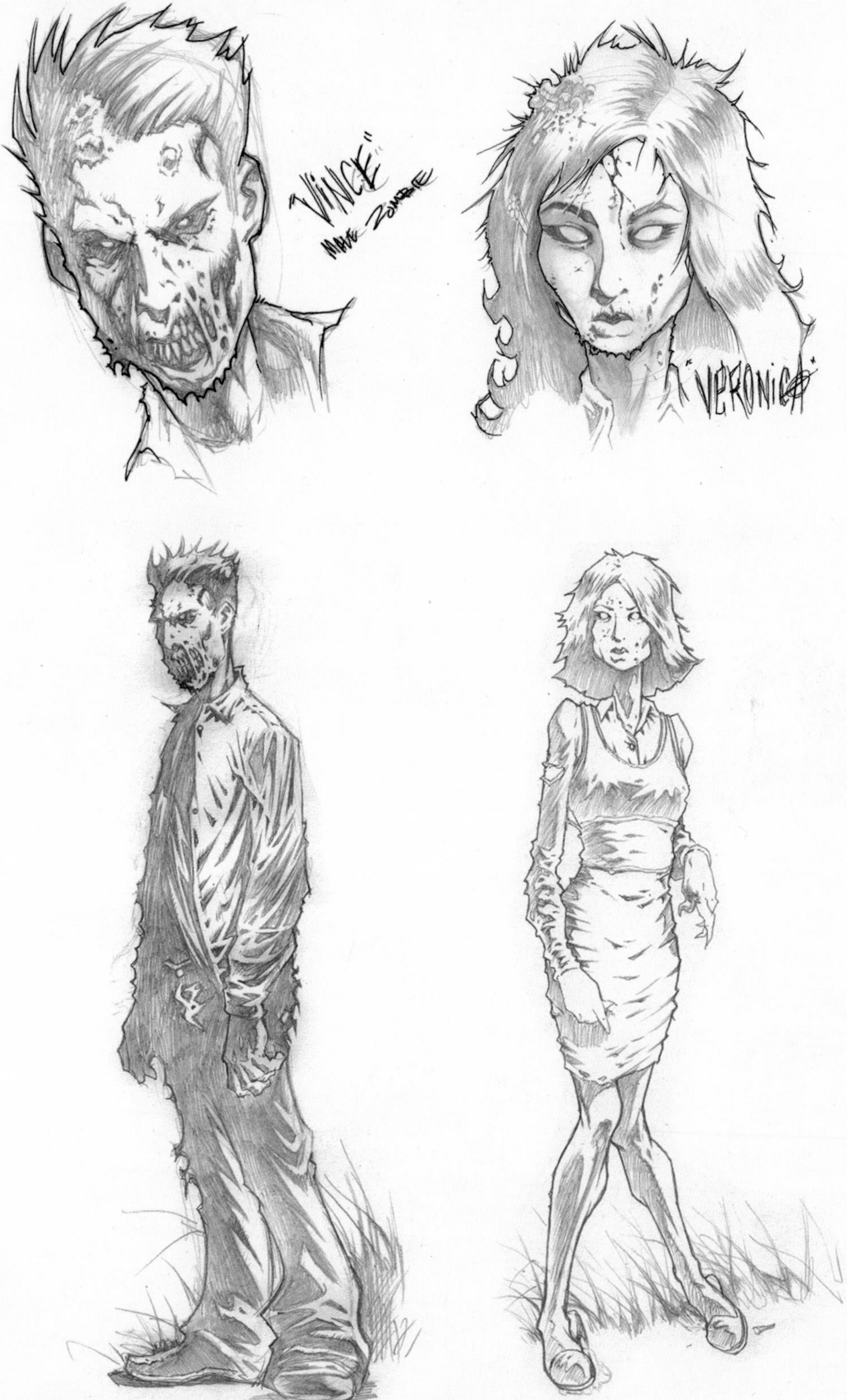
"VINCE"
MALE ZOMBIE
"VERONICA"

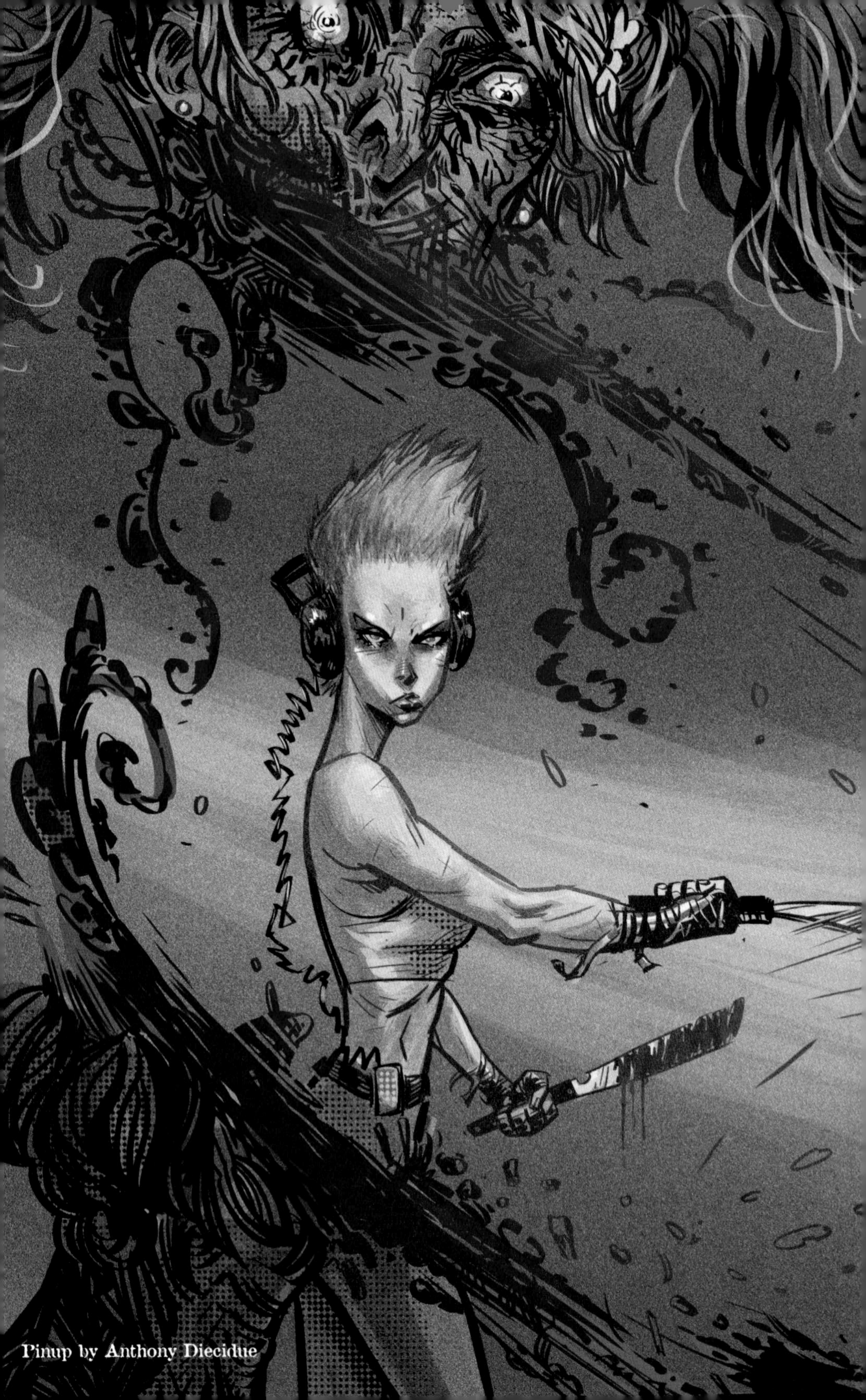

Pinup by Anthony Diecidue

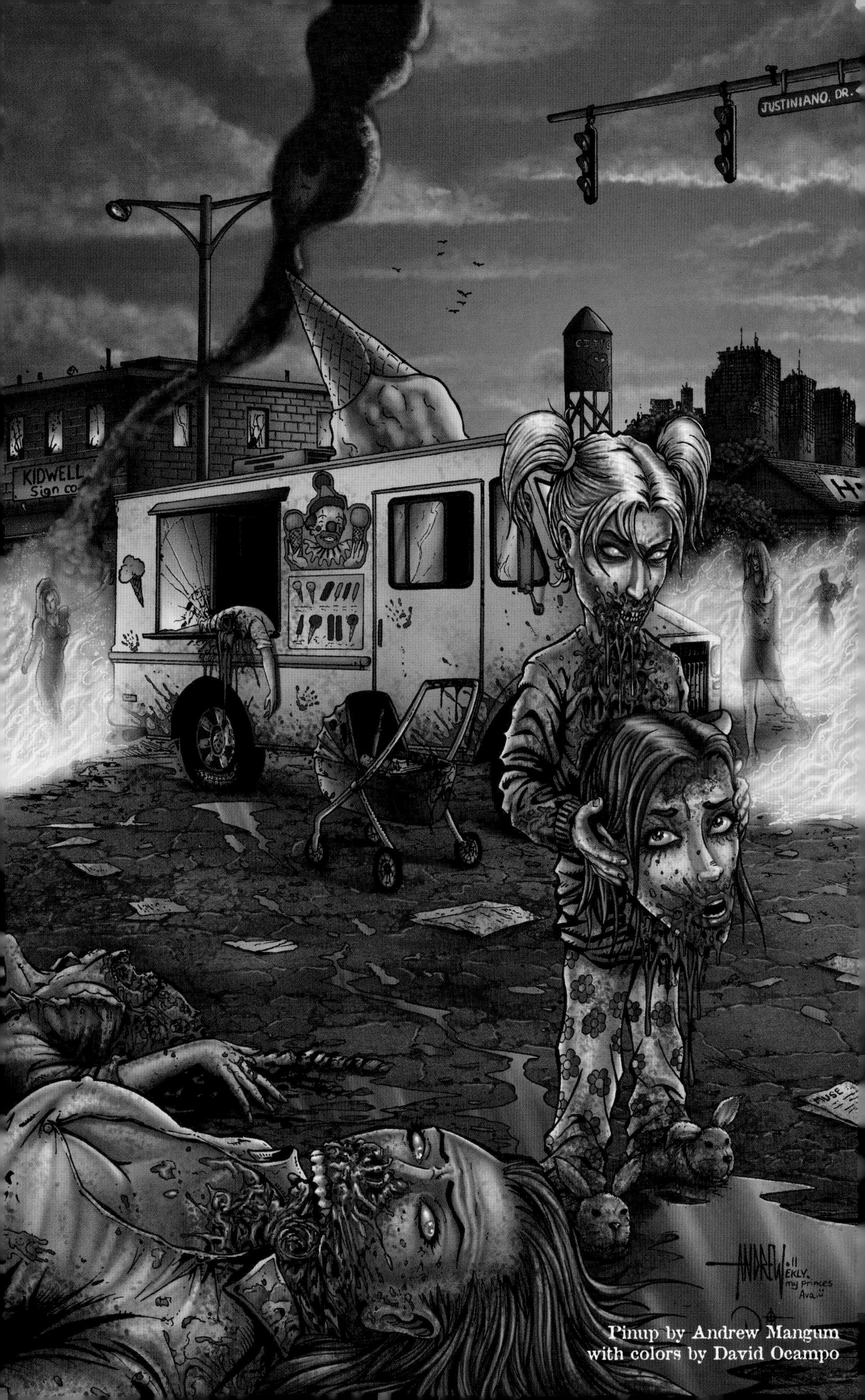
JUSTINIANO. DR.
KIDWELL
Sign co

Pinup by Andrew Mangum
with colors by David Ocampo

Also available from DARK HORSE BOOKS

CREEPY COMICS VOLUME 2: AT DEATH'S DOOR TPB
David Lapham, Jeff Parker, Rick Geary, Patric Reynolds, and others

Continuing the terrifying tradition of the odious original, Dark Horse's *Creepy* brings a modern flavor to classic horror! In this vicious volume, your dear Uncle Creepy presents over a dozen new spine-tingling stories from twisted talents including David Lapham, Jeff Parker, Doug Moench, Joe R. Lansdale, Jason Shawn Alexander, Timothy Truman, Rick Geary, Colleen Coover, Emily Carroll, Nathan Fox, and more! With so much fear to go around, this awful omnibus is sure to keep you drenched in a cold sweat all the way through!

$19.99 • 978-1-59582-951-1

LIVING WITH THE DEAD TPB
Mike Richardson, Ben Stenbeck

Two survivors of a global catastrophe disguise themselves as corpses to survive in a land of the walking dead. Soon the two friends save a lovely young gun-crazy woman named Betty, who becomes a source of rivalry between them. With hundreds of zombies out for a snack, the three try their best to blend in so as not to become the next item on the menu.

$9.99 • 978-1-59307-906-2

R.I.P.D. VOLUME 2: CITY OF THE DAMNED TPB
Jeremy Barlow, Peter M. Lenkov, Tony Parker

Just because Roy Pulsipher and Nick Walker are dead, that doesn't mean their time in law enforcement is over. Roy and Nick are officers in the Rest in Peace Department, sworn to serve the Almighty and protect the living from evil's foul corruption. Their current case has them chasing a ghostly fanatic determined to undo all of creation—a threat with very personal connections to Roy's past, stretching back a hundred years.

$14.99 • 978-1-61655-113-1

THE STRAIN VOLUME 1 TPB
David Lapham, Mike Huddleston

When a Boeing 777 lands at JFK International Airport and goes dark on the runway, the Centers for Disease Control, fearing a terrorist attack, calls in Dr. Ephraim Goodweather and his team of expert biological-threat first responders. Only an elderly pawnbroker from Spanish Harlem suspects a darker purpose behind the event—an ancient threat intent on covering mankind in darkness.

$19.99 • 978-1-61655-032-5

AVAILABLE AT YOUR LOCAL COMICS SHOP OR BOOKSTORE
To find a comics shop in your area, call 1-888-266-4226. For more information or to order direct, visit DarkHorse.com or call 1-800-862-0052 • Mon.–Fri. 9 AM to 5 PM Pacific Time. Prices and availability subject to change without notice.

Creepy™ © New Comic Company. *Living with the Dead*® © Dark Horse Comics, Inc. *R.I.P.D.*™ © Peter M. Lenkov. *The Strain*™ © Guillermo del Toro. All rights reserved.